RAISING COMPASSIONATE, COURAGEOUS CHILDREN IN A VIOLENT WORLD

by
DR. JANICE COHN

LONGSTREET PRESS
Atlanta, Georgia

Published by
LONGSTREET PRESS, INC.
A subsidiary of Cox Newspapers,
A subsidiary of Cox Enterprises, Inc.
2140 Newmarket Parkway
Suite 118
Marietta, GA 30067

Permission to quote from *Why Did It Happen: Helping Children Cope
in a Violent World,* by Janice Cohn, copyright © 1994 by Janice Cohn,
has been granted by Morrow Junior Books, a division of William Morrow
and Company, Inc.

Printed in the United States of America

Printed by Maple-Vail Book Manufacturing

1st printing, 1996

Library of Congress Catalog Card Number: 95-82234
ISBN: 1-56352-276-4

Jacket design by Jill Dible
Book design by Neil Hollingsworth
Cover photograph © Uniphoto/Atlanta

In memory of my father

CONTENTS

ACKNOWLEDGMENTS

This book could not have been written without some very special people.

I first met my editor, Suzanne De Galan, over a rather elegant brunch. As the orange juice was served, I began to talk in general terms about the work I had been doing during the past several years. By the time the check arrived, Suzanne had helped me shape my experiences and ideas into an outline for a book proposal.

At every juncture in this project, I could count on Suzanne for enthusiasm, support, and a wealth of ideas. She was a sounding board, a critic, and, finally, a trusted friend. In short, she is the kind of editor that every author hopes for, and I'm very aware of my luck in finding her.

The Giraffe Project, based in Langley, Washington, is devoted to encouraging children and adults to "stick their necks out" for the common good. When I first found out about this organization, I was immediately intrigued and called its founder and president, Ann Medlock. Our first telephone conversation lasted almost an hour and a half, and it soon became apparent that Ann and I had unknowingly been working toward precisely the same goals, although on different coasts.

For years, the Project has been dauntlessly tracking down "unsung heroes" who have shown genuine moral courage. Upon hearing about my book, Ann immediately offered me the use of the Project's resources, not the least of which was her considerable knowledge in this area. The organization's meticulous files were a treasure trove for me. A.T. Birmingham-Young, who maintains the project's files of heroes with scrupulous accuracy, helped me track down all of the young people and their families who are profiled in this book. If you are a hero, albeit a modest one, don't even attempt to evade A.T.; she will find a way to discover you and your good deeds!

Drs. Ervin Staub, Nancy Eisenberg, and Mark Barnett are nationally recognized researchers who study the development of empathy in children. Despite demanding research, teaching, and writing responsibilities, they spent hours sharing their expert opinions with me and could not have been more generous or supportive. This was true, as well, of the other researchers quoted in the book, whom I spoke to less extensively.

More than 20 years ago, I read a deeply moving book, *Journey,* by Robert and Suzanne Massie. It told of their family's struggle to cope with the consequences of their son Bobby's hemophilia. A book about adversity, courage, and renewal, *Journey* gave *me* courage during a difficult time. Over the years, as I recommended this book to many of my patients, I periodically wondered what had become of Bob Massie. Then, just as I began writing my own book, I picked up *The New York Times* one morning and came upon an article about Bob, who was now Reverend Robert Massie. Reading that article resulted in my finally meeting and interviewing him, as well as his inimitable mother, Suzanne. Both of them, despite many constraints on their busy schedules, have been extraordinarily generous with their time and support. The same has been true of Rabbi Eugene Markovitz, Edwin Santos, Brian and Ruth Jackson, and each of the parents interviewed for the "Exceptional Children...Exceptional Parents" chapter of this book.

Brian and Tammie Schnitzer, Wayne Inman, Margaret E. MacDonald, and Reverend Keith Torney had inspired me before I ever met them. Reading about their actions in a newspaper article, I called Wayne in Billings, Montana, the same day. That phone call led to a trip to Billings, where I was able to meet and talk with Wayne, Tammie, Brian, Margie, and Keith. Those meetings, in turn, resulted in two books, a reevaluation of my own life's priorities, and a continuing friendship with these five remarkable people.

I heard about Andrea Diamond and Suzanne Singer from an informal grapevine that keeps track of people whose creativity and accomplishments have made an impact on children. Andrea and Suzanne were delightful to get to know and have become, over the months, valued friends. Via lunch dates, cellular phones, and faxes, they shared their own experiences with me and gave me a number of additional leads and suggestions. Despite their overpacked schedules, they always found time to keep me "on the straight and narrow" and offer constant support and good cheer.

My friend Lynne Smilow helped me with just about every aspect of this book. She acted as creative adviser, researcher, and interviewer. But what I appreciated most were her unflagging enthusiasm and her ever-present sense of humor. We were both changed by this project, and it was wonderful to be able to discuss what we had learned with each other. Lynne's husband, Jonathan, also got in on the act. There wasn't a single time I spoke with him during the writing of the book when he didn't offer encouragement and ideas of his own.

Mary Riskin is a children's librarian who embodies knowledge, dedication, and a passion for her work. Although children and children's literature are the main focus of her energies, she has always provided crucial help to authors, as well. I have grown accustomed to relying on her sharp critical skills, and now I owe an additional debt of gratitude for the time, effort, and insight that she and her colleague, Maggie Shoemaker, contributed to the listing of children's books contained in the appendix of the book. This list simply could not have been done without their help.

I'd also like to thank John Skillin for his suggestions of recommended family videos listed in the book's appendix. His input was extremely helpful.

Michael Katz is the kind of friend whom everyone should have. His encouragement and patience seem endless, as does his ingenuity. He was supportive and enthusiastic about this book from the beginning, and even located the perfect "borrowed house," where, during the summer of 1995, I wrote much of the book. Thank you, Michael.

Although I don't often get to talk with my two colleagues, Dr. Martin Goldstein and Dr. Earl Grollman, whenever I do see them, they never fail to give me a sense of renewed purpose and determination. Such was the case with the writing of this book. Earl is quoted liberally at several points in the text, and Marvin's sense of direction is apparent throughout.

Jane Clarke Fowkes, despite numerous responsibilities to her job, her family, and her community, carefully read and critiqued the first draft of the book. How she found the time I will never know, but her input has been much appreciated.

I am indebted, as well, to Liz Jaffe for her word-processing skills and her unflappable personality; to the Department of Psychiatry at Newark Beth Israel Medical Center, which, as always, provided help and support; and to friends and family, who somehow always managed to be there whenever I needed them.

Finally, I owe much to the many hundreds of parents and children I've worked with in my more than 20 years as a psychotherapist. Their stories, courage, and determination have touched me in ways that I can never fully describe.

Raising Compassionate, Courageous Children In A Violent World

INTRODUCTION

Children in the U.S. today live in a society that is substantially more violent than any other Western democracy.[1] According to the National Victim Center and the Crime Victims' Research and Treatment Center, a violent crime occurs in our country every 17 seconds, affecting approximately one out of four households.[2]

In addition to the violence that families personally experience each year, certain violent crimes are collectively experienced by our nation as a whole via our televisions, radios, and print media. Consider this: From 1992 to 1996, during the period in which I conceived of, researched, and wrote this book, most of us were alternately saddened, angered, and horrified by the Los Angeles riots; the kidnapping and murder of 12-year-old Polly Klass; Susan Smith's murders of her two small sons; the murder, by a stray bullet, of nine-year-old James Darby, who had written to President

Clinton days before his death, beseeching the president to do something about the crime in his neighborhood; the brutal killings of Nicole Brown and Ronald Goldman; the slaying of Yitzak Rabin; the shocking, senseless slaughter of young schoolchildren in Scotland; and the bombings of the World Trade Center in New York City and the Federal Building in Oklahoma City. This is in addition, of course, to regularly televised stories of murder, deadly hate crimes, drug-related violence, images of death and mutilation in Bosnia, and countless other international tragedies.

Are children aware of violence in the world beyond their own homes and communities, even when adults do not directly discuss it with them? You bet they are.

I've been a practicing psychotherapist working with children and families for the past 23 years. During that period of time, I've been struck by the marked increase in the level of anxiety displayed by many of the youngsters I work with. There are many reasons for this, but much of these children's anxiety has stemmed from their feeling that they live in a dangerous world.

Since the 1994 publication of my children's book, *Why Did It Happen: Helping Children Cope in a Violent World*, I have been going into classrooms in inner-city, middle-class, and affluent suburban schools and talking with children about what it feels like to be living in the world today.

I almost always start with the same question: "There are good things and bad things that happen in this world. What are some of the good things?" Kids then proceed to tell me about their vacation trips, computer games, bicycles, and other goodies they've received. Sometimes, they relate having attained a special dream or goal. Almost everyone has something to tell, and it's usually very personal—things that have happened to them or to the people they know. One seven-year-old, for example, excitedly spoke about her aunt's winning the lottery.

Then I say, "Tell me about some of the bad things that happen." And what I hear, no matter which neighborhood I'm in, are stories about people robbing and killing one another, people bombing buildings, and kids getting shot or kidnapped. I also hear about drugs, AIDS, and domestic abuse. Some of the scariest stories I am told come from children who live very privileged lives and have not personally experienced these dire acts. But they are afraid they might.

"You know that girl in California who got kidnapped when she was home in her own room," one eight-year-old told the group. "Well, I think about her a lot. They say her mom was right in the next room. And this guy came in and had a gun and made her go with him. And her mom was *right there*. The police and everyone are looking for her, and they think she's dead."

I commented that she sounded pretty upset about this.

"Yeah," she nodded. "'Cause if it can happen there it can happen anyplace."

The actual chances of a child's being kidnapped in his or her own home, with a parent present, are infinitesimally small, but try convincing many children of that fact. They don't care about statistics. All they know is what they *feel*.

A number of research studies have been conducted to

assess children's reactions to well-publicized violent events in our society. These events include assassinations, race riots, bombings, killings, and kidnappings. Predictably, such events are found to raise children's anxiety and to color their view of the world.[3] Though their immediate environment might be relatively safe, they often do not feel safe because of events that have taken place far from their home. "Could the people that did it come here?" a seven-year-old New Yorker asked me, shortly after the Oklahoma City bombing.

In one third-grade classroom, in a picture-perfect suburban town, children talked about James Darby, the boy who was killed by a stray bullet.

"That boy, they shouldn't have shot him," one child said. "He didn't do anything. He just wanted them to leave him alone. And so he wrote to President Clinton to make him stop. But before [the president] could do anything, they shot him."

"Who's 'they'?" I asked the class.

"The people in gangs," one child called out.

"All those people that want to hurt little kids," said another student.

"You know, the criminals and bad people," a third child offered.

"And where are these people?" I asked.

Though a few children replied that "they" were "where poor people live," most of the class thought that dangerous people were essentially everywhere.

"You can never tell," one youngster told me solemnly. "They could be anywhere."

What can parents and teachers do to help children cope with these worries? There are many positive things that *can* be done, but often the efforts of caring adults to keep children safe and help them protect themselves breed even more anxiety, along with mistrust and suspicion of others. This, in turn, affects children's capacity to develop into empathic, caring human beings. If children feel those outside their immediate circle are capable of harming them or the people they love, is it likely they will volunteer time, money, and effort to help the very strangers they mistrust?

A Pair of Gloves

Patricia Brent* was walking down a Manhattan street with her daughter, Andrea. She was absentmindedly thinking about what to make for dinner when her curious, exuberant four-year-old brought her abruptly back to the present.

"Mommy, look!" Andrea called out, as she extricated her hand from her mother's.

Patricia saw her daughter run toward the corner, where an apparently homeless gray-haired man was sitting on the sidewalk, dressed in several layers of tattered clothing. Pinned onto his outer sweater was what looked like some kind of military medal. He had positioned a large piece of folded cardboard to partially shield himself from the chilling wind, but it had little effect; his shivering was clearly visible.

Patricia caught up with her daughter just as the girl was

*pseudonym

introducing herself to the man. "Hello. My name is Andrea. What's yours?" There was no answer, but Andrea continued, "How come you're sitting out here in the cold?"

The man nodded. He seemed to be in a daze. Was it drugs or exhaustion? It was hard to tell.

Patricia grasped her daughter's shoulders protectively. "Honey, it's late. We really have to be getting home."

Andrea turned toward her. "But, Mommy, he isn't wearing any gloves. And it's so cold out. Why isn't he wearing gloves?"

It was true. The old man's hands were bare and trembling.

"Mommy, shouldn't he be wearing gloves?"

Patricia shot a look at the man. Eyes glazed, he started fumbling into the paper shopping bag at his side. He seemed to be trying to pull something out. Could it be some sort of weapon? He did look a little deranged.

"Sweetie, we've got to go now," Patricia said more insistently. She was beginning to feel frightened. Looking up, she saw that other pedestrians were walking past without a glance.

"But he looks so cold, Mommy."

Finally, the man found what he was looking for and pulled it out. Wrapped in a crumpled piece of paper was a half-eaten piece of chocolate. He gestured toward Andrea to take it. The child reached out, but before she could grasp the candy, Patricia pulled her back.

"I'm . . . I'm sorry," she mumbled to the unknown man. "She just can't accept this. I'm so sorry . . . so sorry . . . but we have to go." She yanked Andrea's hand and half-pulled her down the street. She would have to explain to her daughter when they got home why she had to be careful. He was, after all, a total stranger.

She turned toward Andrea and saw her accusing look. "He was cold, Mommy. And he had no gloves!"

Patricia spoke about what had happened a few days later, at a parent workshop I was conducting.

"I haven't really had a good night's sleep since," she told the other mothers and fathers. "All kinds of things were going through my mind when Andrea ran up to that old man. Was he crazy? Was he dangerous? Was he ill? One of my best friends is a nurse who works downtown, and she tells me that a lot of these people have tuberculosis. The kind that's very easy to catch.

"I wanted to just snatch my daughter away. I mean, I'm her parent, I love her, it's my responsibility to keep her safe, isn't it?" The other parents nodded sympathetically.

"But on the other hand," she continued earnestly, "Andrea was right. It was freezing cold out. The poor man didn't have any gloves. In fact, he didn't even have a coat. It just wasn't right. Maybe he was a war veteran. He was wearing a medal. Whatever he was, he needed some help. And what was I teaching my daughter? To just walk away; to be afraid. Maybe what I should have done was go with Andrea to the nearest store and help her pick out a pair of gloves for him. Let her know that we have to try to do something when we see someone like that. Not just walk away. Isn't that my responsibility, too? Isn't that the sort of person that I want her to become?"

The group again nodded sympathetically.

"You're right on both counts," a father spoke out. "That's the problem—for all of us. It's a dangerous world out there. We want to keep our kids safe, but we want to raise them with a heart. We don't want to bring up suspicious, mistrustful kids who aren't going to go out of their way to help anyone except maybe themselves." He paused. "To tell you the truth, I'm not sure what the answer is . . . "

◆

There is a consensus in this country that we want our children to be physically safe from harm but also to embody the values we hold (or want to hold) as a society. For example, we want children to be able to:

- love and trust.
- help others in need.
- discern and take a stand against bigotry, hatred, and victimization.
- be sensitive to people's feelings and know how to comfort others who are hurting.
- resist being overwhelmed and discouraged by the violence, callousness, and cynicism that often permeate our society.
- do what is right despite pressures and threats from others.

It's been almost two years since that workshop in which Patricia Brent shared her story, and the basic dilemma for parents continues: Mothers and fathers want to protect their kids from harm, but they want them "to have a heart," too. Although the world hasn't gotten any safer in those two years, more and more is being learned about how to raise kids who are caring and morally courageous *despite* the world they live in. In fact, despite the gloom and doom articulated about our society, despite crime and racial and religious intolerance, despite people's anger and cynicism, there is every reason to be hopeful. Important and surprising research findings are helping us to better understand just how empathy can be effectively nurtured and developed in children. In addition, across the country, special communities, schools, organizations, and committed individuals have taken bold, courageous actions that are inspiring and nurturing young people to be caring and empathic toward others. The first part of this book explores the promise and the practical applications of the most up-to-date research in empathy development. The second part profiles communities and individuals who have inspired and made a positive impact upon children. I believe that these two sections, taken together, provide important lessons for us all.

Part I
SOLUTIONS FOR TROUBLED PARENTS

Chapter One
FOSTERING COMPASSION AND COURAGE

We Americans like to think of ourselves as a caring, compassionate people. The tenets of compassion are taught in Sunday school classes and sermonized regularly in our country's churches, synagogues, and other places of worship. But there is an increasing discrepancy between the reality and the ideal.

According to two recent, wide-ranging surveys,[1] people in the U.S. have become less compassionate about the problems of the poor and minorities and are contributing less money and time to charities than they did a decade or so ago. These studies characterize many Americans as angry and self-absorbed. Other studies indicate that a number of emotional disorders, including depression and anxiety, are on the rise.[2] The reasons for these trends are, of course, complex. Economic uncertainty; violence; ever-widening economic, social, and racial divisions; and multiple stresses on dual-career families, "blended" families, single-parent families; and even that increasingly elusive ideal, the "traditional" two-parent family, all contribute to people's inclination to turn inward and focus on their own problems and concerns.

Yet, despite our society's ills, a core group of people continue to report high levels of well-being and life satisfaction. According to the research, such people frequently report being involved with something beyond themselves; often their actions involve a commitment to helping others and working toward a social ideal.[3] The fact is that when people develop into compassionate, caring human beings, it not only benefits society but also promotes personal happiness and higher self-esteem as well.

This correlation also holds true for children. Researchers generally agree that children who have the capacity to be empathic and caring toward others and the motivation and courage to stand up for what they believe is right perform better socially, academically, and in their adult careers than do children who are not empathic. In addition, there is evidence that children who care about others and are involved, even in small ways, in helping people in need feel better about themselves and are at lower risk of experiencing depression.[4]

This finding is particularly important because, by all accounts, the national rates of childhood depression and attempted suicide are steadily rising.[5] Caring for and about others and being less focused on oneself has always been regarded as an effective antidote for adults and children in countering depression and other emotional disorders. Now this theory has been confirmed by a major university research study involving more than 400 people of various ages.[6]

In addition to depression, another national mental-health concern is the troubling rise in narcissistic disorders diagnosed by mental-health professionals today. Narcissism has been called the psychiatric affliction of the '80s and '90s. Some social commentators have noted that we are becoming a nation of narcissists.

The dictionary defines narcissism as self-love. The phenomenon derives its name from the beautiful youth in Greek mythology who becomes hopelessly infatuated with his own reflection. Self-love, we are told by psychological theorists, is crucial in developing self-esteem. In order to be able to truly love others, we must first be able to love ourselves. But the question is, How much?

As a psychotherapist and school consultant, I have found that in an effort to bolster children's self-esteem, parents and teachers sometimes tend to lavish them with praise and compliments for very modest accomplishments that don't represent the children's best efforts. However, such excessive praise does not necessarily foster higher achievement and pride. Instead, it can promote an unhealthy narcissism that encourages children to feel "entitled" to such praise without having earned it.

The key to making children feel good about themselves and develop a healthy sense of self-esteem, researchers are discovering, is not to give children empty praise and compliments but rather to work with youngsters to enable them to experience *genuine* accomplishment. That might mean achieving a goal (virtually any goal), developing a talent, or **"making a difference" by contributing time and effort to helping others who are in need.**

Clearly, when children are involved in helping others,

they are ultimately helping themselves. The question is, what can parents and other caring adults do to encourage children to develop into compassionate, altruistic human beings? In the past, adults had little concrete information to guide them. That situation is now changing, as researchers are discovering specific actions that can have a positive and profound impact upon young people. Following is an exploration of these findings, along with the researchers' comments and suggestions.

SHOW CHILDREN THAT THEY ARE LOVED AND CHERISHED

Dr. Ervin Staub, one of this country's premier researchers studying the development of empathy in children, has a simple message for parents: The key factor that determines whether children develop into caring, compassionate human beings is parental love.

"Children need to be treated with affection, respect, and benevolence," he says. "They need to feel secure in the knowledge that their parent (or parent substitute) cares about their well-being and will protect and care for them. Children's perceptions of their world and the people in it are formed by their own experiences of how they are treated by the people closest to them. They will treat others as they themselves have been treated."[7]

Dozens of research studies bear out Dr. Staub's conclusion. There is convincing evidence that children whose parents are openly affectionate with them and respond sensitively to their emotional needs are more likely to develop into individuals whom researchers rate as genuinely sensitive to others' feelings than are children whose parents are not nurturing and affectionate.

On the other hand, parents who try to discipline children by withdrawing love, threatening physical force, or humiliating or embarrassing them raise youngsters who have great difficulty feeling compassion for others.[8] This finding underscores the widely accepted conclusion among researchers and clinicians that when it comes to disciplining children, the end never justifies the means. If a child makes a remark or engages in an action that is cruel or insensitive to another person, it is completely counterproductive to then be cruel and insensitive to the child as a punishment.

Matthew,* age six, looks with fascination at the woman seated at the table next to him and his mother in the neighborhood ice-cream parlor.

"Look, Mommy, she's so fat," he exclaims loudly. His mother shoots him a stern warning look, which he proceeds to ignore. "She's even fatter than that man we saw on TV yesterday, remember? She's the fattest person I ever saw!"

Clearly the woman has heard him. Looking distinctly uncomfortable, a crimson flush begins to spread across her face. Matthew's mother, deeply embarrassed, starts to yell at her son. "Matthew, shut up this instant. I don't want to hear you say another word!"

"But, Mommy," her son begins to protest.

"Not one word! Didn't you hear me?" Her voice is rising. She can hear it, but all she can think of is the obese

*Matthew and Denise are fictitious composites of children whose parents have attended my workshops.

young woman at the next table. She can't risk her son's making another hurtful remark.

"If you don't know how to behave when I take you to a restaurant, there won't be any more trips to get ice cream. I thought you knew better. When you get home, you're going to get a taste of just how angry I am!" That silences Matthew, who is aware that several other customers are looking right at him. He pushes away his dish of ice cream and announces sullenly, "I don't want any of this stuff, anyway."

Denise feels the same kind of upset as Mathew. She refuses to share her new game with her playmate Amanda, though her father has pointed out that Amanda doesn't have many toys of her own. When Amanda persists in trying to play with Denise's new game, Denise hits her in the head. Hard. To make matters worse, she refuses to apologize. "No!" she tells her father when he insists that she do so.

"I'm not talking to you or even looking at you until you say you're sorry," he responds to Denise's defiant answer. "Where do you come off thinking you can act like this? You can just sit in your room all day if you want to be stubborn."

Denise still refuses to utter a word, but her eyes fill with tears. "I don't care about those tears," her father tells her coldly. "Now get away from me and go right to your room. I don't want you near me!"

Dr. Mark Barnett of Kansas State University, an expert on the development of empathy in children, says the consequences of withdrawing love as a punishment for misbehavior can be grave: "It's devastating for children to think that their parents do not love them, or might withhold that love if they do something wrong. They need to feel secure in the fact that they are cared for and loved despite their mistakes and misbehaviors. This makes it possible for children to develop an inner security that their own emotional needs will be taken care of. It's *only then* that they can learn to be responsive to the emotional needs of others."[9]

In the course of Dr. Staub's research, he recently conducted an experiment that underscored the connection between children's need to feel secure and their desire and ability to help others. "In this study," he explains, "I did something as simple as have adults either interact with children in a warm and affectionate way or in a totally indifferent way; not hostile or negative, just indifferent. Later on, in an adjoining room, there was a loud crash and sounds of distress. The children who had been treated with warmth and affection were more likely to go into the other room to investigate and see if they could help than were the children who were treated with indifference.

"The adults who had interacted with the children in this experiment had been strangers. The children did not know them. But it did not take too much time for the children to feel safe in the environment we had created when the adults treated them with kindness and respect."[10]

GIVE GUIDELINES FOR ACCEPTABLE AND UNACCEPTABLE BEHAVIOR

Though love is a crucial foundation upon which children's moral development is built, love is not enough. Children also need understandable and consistent guidelines for acceptable and unacceptable behavior toward others. Research studies have repeatedly shown that parental love and affection must be accompanied by such guidelines, and that these guidelines must be strictly enforced.

Dr. Nancy Eisenberg of Arizona State University has produced a number of important studies on the development of empathy in children. In an interview with *The New York Times*, she emphasized that "warmth is the background that makes other things parents do effective, but warmth alone is not enough to develop empathy . . . . In fact, warmth alone can encourage selfishness in a child. Children need a firm parental hand in setting limits and guidelines."[11] Eisenberg has found that parents who are loving but permissive and who do not set limits on their children's behavior toward others have children who tend to be more selfish and less inclined to help others than are youngsters whose parents provide more discipline.

Help Children Understand the Consequences of Their Actions

Researchers generally agree on the importance of helping children understand the impact of their actions upon others. Dr. Staub explains: "Very specifically tell them that this is good to do, and this is not good to do; this is acceptable and this is not acceptable. The research indicates that it is crucial to talk with children and explain the reasons for all of this. Why is it that the child should not take that toy? Why is it that he or she must share that toy? Explain things in terms of the consequences of children's behavior toward other people.

"Explaining consequences means focusing on how the other person will feel if a child acts in a certain way. For example, the person's feelings will be hurt, they will be angry, they will be embarrassed, they will feel rejected. Don't focus on abstract principles—talk about people's emotions."[12]

If we go back to Matthew and his mother and re-create the scene in a different way, incorporating this concept, the interchange might go something like this: Matthew, fascinated by the appearance of an obese woman sitting at a nearby table in a restaurant, exclaims loudly, "Look, Mommy, she's so fat!" His mother shoots him a warning look, trying to signal that Matthew should not make such a public comment about the woman's appearance, but her son ignores her and goes on blithely, commenting: "She's even fatter than that man we saw on TV yesterday, remember? She's the fattest person I ever saw!"

Clearly the object of his remarks has heard him. She looks distinctly uncomfortable, as a crimson flush begins to spread across her face. "Matthew," his mother says softly but sternly, "you mustn't say anything more about how that woman looks. Some people feel very sensitive about their weight. When people say things about it, it makes them feel bad and embarrasses them. I know that's not something you would want to do, is it?"

Matthew shakes his head no and resumes eating his ice cream.

HELP CHILDREN PUT THEMSELVES IN OTHERS' PLACES

Virtually all researchers have found that in order to learn empathy, children must be able to put themselves in others' places. Ask your children how they would feel if someone did something to embarrass or hurt or humiliate them. This technique helps children develop a sensitivity to others' feelings. Moreover, it is much more effective than ordering a child to do something because it is "the right thing to do," or because a parent or another authority figure "says so." The issue should not be "obedience"; it should be understanding another person's pain. If we re-create the scenario between Denise and her father with this concept in mind, it might go as follows:

Denise refuses to share her new game with Amanda. Her father explains to her that Amanda does not have many toys of her own, but this explanation falls on deaf ears. Denise wants to play with her new game herself, and she wants to play with it *now*. When Amanda persists in trying to share the game, Denise feels that a hit on the head will make her point nicely, and she hits Amanda. Hard.

Denise's father then takes her aside and tells her sternly that he cannot allow her to hit Amanda. He knows she is upset, but how would she feel if Amanda hit her? She wouldn't like it, would she? In fact, he'd bet she'd be pretty angry, just as the glaring Amanda is right now.

He then tells her again that Amanda doesn't have many toys of her own. Denise is lucky; she has lots and lots of toys. Can she imagine how she would feel to have practically no toys at all? Does she think that maybe, if that were the case, she would want to play with her friends' toys when she went on a play date?

Denise, being only five years old, is still very much focused on her own needs. She still does not want to relinquish her new game. "But I just got it *yesterday*," she protests.

"Well, then, what can we do?" her father asks her. "If you were Amanda, what would *you* want you to do?"

"I don't want her to play with my new game. But maybe she can play with this," she says, pointing to another favorite game.

"That's a good idea," her father tells her. "Let's go talk with Amanda."

This technique can be equally effective in helping children develop sensitivity and compassion toward people who are "different" in some way. One of the most difficult and debilitating effects of a physical handicap or chronic illness is the social isolation that often ensues. Often children don't know what to say or how to act with those who are ill or handicapped. Could such a thing happen to them? Is it catching? Is the other child weird? What would the other kids think if they extended a gesture of friendship?

If your child has a classmate with a physical handicap, and your child makes fun of that classmate's odd appearance because she is in a wheelchair or has thick, strange-looking glasses or no hair because of chemotherapy treatments, don't punish him for his insensitivity or lecture him about why he has to be kind. Ask him how he thinks *he* would feel if he were that person and people made those remarks to him. Then go beyond that and ask him to imagine what it would be like to feel isolated and alone. Talking to children about the loneliness that others may feel not only promotes understanding, it often prompts children to help in a meaningful way, perhaps by stopping by a classmate's or neighbor's house to say hello, perhaps by remembering to include that child in a social activity. These kinds of acts give kids the same satisfaction and empowerment that adults experience in similar situations.

PRIMARILY DISCIPLINE THROUGH REASONING

Researchers agree that the use of reasoning and discussion as disciplinary tools is one of the most effective methods of fostering children's positive moral development. Highly authoritarian disciplinary methods, in which parents impose rules on children without explaining the reasons for them and then expect unquestioning obedience, are often counterproductive. A university study involving more than 100 children and their parents found that disciplining children in an authoritarian way tended to stifle their initiative, creativity, and intellectual curiosity.[13] It's important to note, however, that the authoritarian model described above is an extreme one. No researchers or clinicians suggest that parents should not exert authority or make key decisions about their children's welfare. However, when children are given explanations for household rules and are allowed to voice their opinions, and even disagree (though the parents have the last word), research suggests that they become more adept at exercising social skills, relating to others, and coping with life's problems.[14]

Clearly, the use of reasoning is important in helping children develop the capacity for empathy. Nevertheless, parents should not underestimate the power of emotion in positively influencing their children's ability to care about others. In an interesting study involving mothers and preschool children,[15] mothers were asked to describe how they reacted to their children's responses to the distress of others. The study concluded that young children who displayed a high degree of empathy toward others had mothers who conveyed a clear message to their children about the consequences of their behavior toward others and communicated this with intense emotion. As Dr. Carolyn Zahn-Wexler, the primary investigator in this study, pointed out, the mothers' obvious emotion let the children know the depth of their feelings about the issue. At a very young age, when children's primary concern is pleasing their parents, this kind of passionate response makes a powerful impression on children that they are likely to remember as they grow older— *if* their parents and other caregivers maintain that passion and conviction about their beliefs. Parents can communicate such passion not just through words but through expression and body language. Young children, who are just beginning to learn to express themselves verbally, are very quick to pick up on nonverbal symbols.

SHOW CHILDREN BY EXAMPLE HOW TO TREAT OTHERS

Throughout history, during times of persecution, oppression, and lawlessness, there have been certain people who have had the moral courage to speak out and take a stand, despite the risks.

For decades, researchers have tried to understand what motivates these people to act. Is it something in their backgrounds or psychological makeup that enables people to risk intimidation, ostracism, physical injury, and sometimes even death?

Parental Role Models

Though each person is unique, one crucial common denominator that investigators found in their studies of people who showed unusual courage and compassion was the strong influence that role models—particularly their parents and parent-substitutes—played in their lives.

In *The Altruistic Personality*, a comprehensive 1988 study examining rescuers of Jews in Nazi Europe,[16] Drs. Samuel and Pearl Oliner concluded that the actions of these rescuers, who often literally risked their lives because they thought it was "the right thing to do," were largely prompted and sustained by the values taught them by their parents' words and deeds.

Dr. David Rosenhan, who has been conducting ongoing research for more than 20 years to determine what prompts altruistic and compassionate behavior, has arrived at the same conclusion, finding that altruism is often profoundly influenced by parental models.

In his study of dedicated, longtime civil-rights leaders, for example, Rosenhan discovered that they had been inspired and nurtured by qualities their parents exemplified, such as courage, perseverance, and a genuine concern for others.[17] Studies by other researchers arrive at similar conclusions.

In today's society, for a variety of reasons, children often don't have those kinds of role models. In a *New York Times* interview, Dr. Rosenhan explained: "Altruism and courage are often connected issues; they are part of the right thing to do. There was a time when we did this. But now, kids don't see these qualities in their parents or teachers. Everyone is sort of getting along, trying to stay out of trouble and make ends meet."[18]

Recently, Dr. Rosenhan elaborated on this thinking: "There are fewer opportunities today for people to show courage because, in part, the times we live in are less dramatic than in the past. The moral battles we grapple with are less fraught with danger. Nowadays, we are not fighting the Nazis or McCarthyism or legalized segregation. The evils we face tend to be less defined, and the consequences for fighting these evils are no longer possible death or injury or economic ruin."[19]

While this period in history may not offer the same dramatic opportunities for courageous actions as did the past, parental modeling continues to be a crucial factor in children's moral development. And researchers and clinicians are concerned about how parents are being affected by living in a world that is often violent and unpredictable. Dr. Marian Radke Yarrow, a prominent researcher in the field of childhood empathy, voiced this concern: "In American culture you could take the position that we're fostering the attitude that being empathic or altruistic is too dangerous."[20]

Dr. Staub, who has extensively studied the factors that prompt people to help one another, agrees with Dr. Rosenhan in identifying parental modeling as a crucial factor in children's moral development. He, along with Dr. Yarrow, worries about how today's parents are being affected by the pressure of living in an often violent and unpredictable world. "The reality is," he explains, "we live in a world that is more dangerous for children. Because of this, parents are more apt to teach children to be careful, to watch out, and to be suspicious and concerned about how people behave toward them. But when parents do that, they create a separation between the child and other people. Children are likely to pull back and be self-protective. As adults train children to be more cautious, it makes them feel less connected to a wide range of people.

"So is there a way we can teach children to be careful and mindful of safety without losing their connectedness to others? Yes, and I believe it is essential that we do that. Parents must be prevailed upon to promote kindness and caring, and to basically represent people as valuable and worthwhile, while at the same time making children aware that there are people who are dangerous. We must help children to learn discrimination rather than promote a blanket withdrawal from other people, or a blanket suspiciousness." [21]

Discriminating between good people and potentially dangerous people is a difficult concept for young children to grasp. But parents and other caring adults can help children begin the process of understanding by emphasizing that while there are many good people in this world, there are also people whom children must be wary of. Teach them, for example, to:

- be careful of strangers and not to accept presents from them or go anywhere with them, no matter how nice they may be.
- be careful of people they know who are acting differently than usual, who are talking or walking strangely, or doing anything to frighten them. If this happens, tell another adult.
- never listen to anyone who tells them to do something they know is wrong, such as hurt someone, lie, steal, or destroy property.

But while cautioning children, remember to add that if a person—whether it's someone they know or a stranger—seems to be hurting or in trouble, they should tell an adult so that that person can be helped. The goal is to keep children safe but capable of caring.

Let's look back at Patricia Brent's story, "A Pair of Gloves," in the introduction to this book. Had Patricia Brent successfully communicated the guidelines just outlined to her daughter, Andrea would not have reached for the chocolate from the homeless man but would still have wanted to help him get a pair of gloves. As Dr. Staub points out: "People who are trusting do not have to be gullible. People who are trusting do not have to close their eyes to clues that indicate someone is not so trustworthy. It's important to teach children to judge people by their actions rather than their words. But it is desirable to generate a basic orientation that is trusting, and within that context to enable children to use their judgment. This is good for both children and our society."[22]

Dr. Staub's point underscores the power that parents have to influence their children's view of the world. **The reality is, no matter how difficult and frightening the world may be, parents have never lost the potential to inspire and influence their children.**

Children Respond

In 1989, under the auspices of the Association of Teachers in Independent Schools in New York City and Vicinity, hundreds of questionnaires were distributed to elementary, middle-, and high-school students, asking them to explain their concept of heroism and to identify whom they considered to be their role models or heroes. This was done as preliminary research for a "Heroes Project" I had originally developed for the New York City Board of Education, and which is now being piloted by the Newark, New Jersey school system.

More than 300 children filled out and returned the questionnaires. Although many spoke of movie stars, sports celebrities, and financial moguls (remember, this was the 1980s), a large proportion of these young people spoke about being influenced and inspired by their parents.

Following are just some of their comments:

> "My first hero is my mom. If she hadn't been there, I might have starved and died of hunger. She also helps to solve my problems and most of all she loves me, and that is enough for a heroine. My second hero is my dad. He's always been there for me, and he loves me also. He is very

kind and he never yells."
(**female fourth grader**)

"My mother is my hero. She showed me right from wrong and was there when I needed her. She really cares. When my mother and father went to an animal kennel and adopted a dog about to be put to sleep, I thought that they were heroes. (I'll bet the dog did, too.)"
(**female fourth grader**)

"My father is also my hero. He taught me to ride a bike, play ball, and showed me how to open the side door on our van."
(**female fifth grader**)

"The people I think are heroes are my mom and dad. You see, my mom is a nurse and my dad is a doctor and they help save lives no matter what."
(**male fifth grader**)

"I think my mother is a heroine because she puts up with my father."
(**male sixth grader**)

"My dad is a hero because he's kind, understanding, smart, strong, wise, and has a good outlook on life. My mom has all the same qualities (except strong)."
(**male seventh grader**)

"My heroes are my mom, my dad, not my sister, and my cat Creamy. He (my cat) was there for me when I cried

(and licked up my tears and made me feel better). He was also there for me when I needed to lean on him for help. My parents were there for the same reasons, and others too (not licking though)."
(female seventh grader)

"My parents are two heroes. They are great people. They try their best at everything, and they help others. Although they make mistakes, all around they are good."
(male eighth grader)

"My mother is my hero because she is so good and unselfish. She doesn't try to show how good she is, she is content to be good and go unrecognized."
(male 11th grader)

"I feel my mother is a heroine, because she is always trying to make my life better. She came from picking cotton to making herself a pretty successful woman today. She really doesn't have the money to send me to private school but she does, anyway, by working day and night. I feel my father is a hero because he also tries very hard, and works very hard to keep me in this private school so life will be easier for me when I get out of school, and I can try to make something out of myself."
(female 11th grader)

"I think of my grandmother as a heroine. She managed to all but raise her sister and brother when her mother was sick, which was about five years. She also managed to put her sister through college while working for the city. To

me, she is the greatest person I know. She has overcome many obstacles in her life and never once has she blamed anyone for these obstacles."
(male 11th grader)

I was especially touched by the words of a fifth grader with whom I spoke informally. She was a scholarship student at one of the most prestigious private schools in Manhattan. Living in an aging housing project in Harlem, Vicky* commuted daily to the city's ritzy upper East Side. She had a heavy academic load, as well as a daunting array of after-school activities. She felt she had to prove herself, she said. People were nice to her, but Vicky didn't really feel as if she fit in. With two younger brothers and a mother who worked two jobs, Vicky faced a number of household chores and baby-sitting duties when she got home from school. Yet despite this, she had volunteered, through her church, to tutor first and second graders in reading skills.

"But how do you have the time to do all this?" I asked her.

"I make the time," she told me simply. "You see, it's the kind of thing my mom's been doing since I can remember. If someone's in trouble or needs something, she's always there. We never had very much, but what we did have, she always shared. She didn't make a big deal about it. She just did it. She's a nurse's aide. And it seems people were forever in our apartment, with scrapes and cuts and all kinds of symptoms. She never sent even one person away. I see the difference that she makes, and how other

*pseudonym

people feel about her. That's what I want to be like—what I think I can be like."

GIVE CHILDREN FREQUENT OPPORTUNITIES TO PERFORM SMALL ACTS OF KINDNESS

Research strongly supports the theory that engaging in small or limited acts of kindness and compassion often leads people to undertake more expansive and sustained acts of altruism than would otherwise have been the case, though this may not have been their original intention.

This phenomenon has been documented by Drs. Samuel and Pearl Oliner in their previously cited study of rescuers of Jews in Nazi Europe. A significant number of rescuers who were interviewed said they had at first planned to offer only limited or temporary help. But their involvement grew. One example is the now well-known case of Oskar Schindler, whose story was movingly written by Thomas Keneally[23] and dramatized by Steven Spielberg in his celebrated film *Schindler's List*.

The Oliners and other researchers offer many additional examples. In *The Altruistic Personality*, a Dutch rescuer recalls:

> In July 1942 we heard that they were going to start picking up Jewish boys aged sixteen and up. Mrs. V.'s sister had a boy of sixteen, and I was very worried about him. Before I was married I had worked for Dr. V. in Amsterdam as a dental assistant, and since [then] we had become friends.

On Sunday, July 11, we went to the V.'s to visit and asked them what Johnny was going to do. She said, "My brother-in-law says maybe it will be just work camps. Maybe it will be good for the boy." And I said, "How stupid can he get?! We know several people who said they are destroying them." So they said, "What can we do?" I said, "Well, we have a home—a downstairs bedroom and bathroom. Why don't you all come over to our place?" We all thought it would be a matter of three weeks; instead it became nearly three years. [24]

For several years, Dr. Staub has studied the effects of exposing children to opportunities that enable them to help others. "One of my major concerns is how we learn as a result of our own actions," he says. "For example, when we get children involved in helping others, it tends to influence other areas of their lives. I've conducted research where I've gotten children to make toys for disadvantaged, hospitalized youngsters. We found that children who were involved in this activity tended to become more helpful in their everyday lives. This was particularly true if the effect of these children's actions on the people they helped was specifically pointed out to them.

"The research shows that people who initially become involved in helping behavior, intending to help in a very limited way, often unexpectedly become committed to what they are doing and end up helping in very extensive ways. People can change as a result of their own actions. We become more concerned about the welfare of the people we help, and also come to see ourselves as more helpful and more willing to help. This in turn makes us more likely to help others in the future.

"Keep in mind that where children are concerned, there is evidence that it's important to introduce them to helping behavior by choosing a few projects with which they can be involved in an ongoing way. For example, take household activities. If one day you say to Johnnie, 'Come help set the table,' and then the next day say, 'I want you to take out the garbage,' it would have a less beneficial effect than if Johnnie were given the same daily responsibilities. Cross-cultural studies have found that children in societies where they have ongoing duties, such as taking care of animals or taking care of younger siblings, are more altruistic and more helpful than children in societies where they have fewer of these responsibilities. Parents should be aware of this when assigning chores to children. The rule of thumb is that chores should be well defined, ongoing, and, at least in some part, connected to others. For example, along with cleaning his or her room, it would be helpful for a child to participate in caring for younger sibings or the family pet."[25]

Mary Ann,* six and a half years old, was responsible for the care of her pet turtle, whom she had named Angel Bunny. (Mary Ann had originally wanted a rabbit as a pet and had never felt entirely satisfied with the compromise she had made with her parents.) Soon she began to lose interest in her pet, who was neither fuzzy, capable of hopping, nor particularly angelic, despite his name. In truth, Angel Bunny did not do much of any-

*pseudonym

thing. Rather somber, even for a turtle, he provided little in the way of amusement. Mary Ann began to find it hard to remember to feed Angel Bunny. "You do it," she tried to convince her mother, and suggested several alternate chores she could do that were more to her liking. Setting the table, she argued, was more grown-up; emptying the dryer, she pointed out, was more fun. Finally, when her parents remained unmoved, she became desperate and offered to take out the garbage (but not every night).

Giving in to Mary Ann's pleas was tempting to her overworked parents. It would have been so much easier to feed the turtle and not have to listen to Mary Ann's whining. But instead, they insisted that she continue to be responsible for Angel Bunny. He was her pet and he was a living thing, deserving of proper care and attention. Mary Ann had to understand that indifference or callousness toward a pet would not be tolerated in their household. No matter what, that particular chore would continue to be hers.

Years later, as an adolescent, Mary Ann remembered that experience. "I never did like that turtle very much. And you know, my parents liked him even less. But they wouldn't let me get rid of him. Even after I found a kid in my class who was willing to trade a perfectly good kazoo for Angel Bunny, my parents wouldn't give in. 'Your pet's a living thing,' my mother insisted. 'We don't trade away or throw away living things.' I remember being furious that night—I really had wanted that kazoo. But I stuck it out and took care of Angel Bunny until he died a peaceful death.

And then, when that boring old smelly turtle died, I realized how odd it felt not to be taking care of . . . something . . . someone. I don't know. I couldn't have a dog or a cat; the apartment building where we lived didn't allow them. And I knew I didn't want another turtle. But in a funny kind of way, Angel Bunny was probably partly responsible for my ending up here [at a neighborhood school] doing volunteer tutoring with these kids."

Emerging research and growing support for children's character education have prompted many schools throughout the country to require children to engage in some type of community service. But Dr. Eisenberg has words of caution for both parents and educators:

"It's important that youngsters not feel coerced into engaging in compulsory community service. There is evidence that if children feel they are being 'forced' to engage in kind, altruistic acts, they attribute the consequences of their behavior to external factors and therefore don't think of themselves as helpful. They're doing what they're doing—they believe—because they have to.

"But you can get kids to engage in this kind of behavior without feeling they are being pressured, by using various subtle and diplomatic means. And you can give them choices, letting them decide the type of activities they would like to engage in. This helps to make it a more meaningful experience for them. Under these circumstances, the research indicates that there is definitely some positive effect on adolescents who are involved in community service. They see themselves as more competent and feel they are achieving something important.

"There is some experimental data that shows these kinds of school activities might be beneficial for children in the younger grades as well. Ervin Staub and I did a study with very young children and found that they didn't yet have a very strong concept of themselves. So engaging in helping behavior didn't initially have much of an impact on their concept of themselves as helpers. However, by the second grade it did start to have an effect. So it's entirely possible that if you give young children opportunities to help others, it may not affect their behavior or self-concept immediately but may have a cumulative effect as they get older, providing them with concrete skills for helping others and a more positive self-image." [26]

USE EVERYDAY MOMENTS TO FOSTER COMPASSION AND CARING

"There's not a day goes by that doesn't offer 'teachable moments' for children," says Dr. Earl Grollman, a nationally known expert in crisis intervention and a former rabbi. "Each day provides opportunities—some small thought or act of compassion—that can be talked about with youngsters. For example, if you watch television tonight with your kids, you'll see something, maybe a piece about Bosnia on the evening news. Your children can write a letter, to let some of the children in Bosnia know they're thinking about them. That's what people need to know—that they're not forgotten.

"When there is a happy occasion in the family, the family can as a rule make a small contribution to charity, as both a kind of thank-you for good fortune and a recognition that others are not as blessed. In many families this becomes a tradition that the children eventually pass on to their own children.

"Or, if you are able to do volunteer work in your community, you can bring your children with you, if at all possible. If you're clearing an elderly neighbor's driveway after a snowstorm, take your children and let them bring a little shovel. If you're bringing food or medicine to someone in the neighborhood, take your children and let them bring a gift of their own, perhaps a special drawing or a clay figure. If you're doing something for the environment, take your children and let them help in some way by planting or weeding or helping to clear rubbish.

"When children experience the joy and satisfaction of realizing that they have the power to touch other people's lives and can make those lives better, even in small ways, it's more effective than any parental lectures or Sunday school lessons can ever be. I've learned this through literally hundreds of discussions with kids."[27]

During the days following the bombing in Oklahoma City, children were inundated day and night with media images of the carnage. They saw lifeless babies being carried out of the rubble and viewed countless interviews with survivors and relatives of the dead. Shortly afterward, I spoke with several dozen elementary-school children about the tragedy. Some of them were noticeably shaken by what they had seen and heard, while others showed no apparent upset, evidencing instead a curious lack of emotion that is often a sign in children of emotional overload. The children expressed sadness for the victims—especially the children—but, predictably, they were mainly concerned about whether something like that could happen to them, their family, or their town. Were they safe?

This was a particularly understandable response from the children who lived in my own town, Montclair, New Jersey. Barely one month earlier, our quiet, pretty, suburban community had been the scene of another tragedy. A former postal employee burst into the local satellite post office, a tiny storefront where two much-beloved postal workers ministered to the community's needs. He then stole thousands of dollars and brutally shot to death the two workers along with two customers. A fifth customer was also shot and sustained life-threatening wounds.

The town went into collective shock, outrage, and grief. As the community's children watched and listened, trying to make sense of what was impossible to understand, their parents and teachers tried to comfort and reassure them. "He was a very sick man," the adults said. "This is a terrible, tragic thing that happened. But such things are very rare. You will be safe. We will protect you."

The children listened but couldn't be totally reassured. How could they be sure such a thing wouldn't happen again?

A few weeks later came Oklahoma City.

As children expressed their feelings about the bombing, their fears and anxieties were apparent. But when we began to talk about what they could do to help and comfort the families of those who had been hurt, I could see their sense of helplessness begin to lessen. Some of the children had already sent cards and drawings to Oklahoma. Others had donated their allowance—in some cases several weeks' worth of allowance—to the Red Cross to help the victims. Still others came up with different ideas: Perhaps they could plant a flower or even a tree, as President and Mrs. Clinton had suggested, or send messages on audiotapes to the wounded children. These were ways in which the children could help themselves gain some mastery over a frightening, incomprehensible event. These children's actions also helped promote a recognition that when others are hurting—no matter who they are—we all have an obligation to reach out and help.

Hours after the bombing, Dr. Grollman traveled to Oklahoma City to help the victims' families. He spent many days at a little church near the bombing site, ministering to the survivors and the rescuers.

When he returned home to Massachusetts, he talked with members of his community about what they could do to help. He spoke about the victims, of course, but he talked as well about the rescuers.

"I told story after story about the rescuers," Dr. Grollman recalls. "Men and women working day and night, under the most unimaginable pressure, to try and save other human beings. The children wrote letters and drew pictures for them, so they would know they were not forgotten, and that their sacrifices and heroism were appreciated.

"I wanted the children to remember those rescuers, and think of them when people talked of the bombers and the hate groups. Because, yes, there is violence and tragedy in this world, but there is goodness and courage, too. Violence may always be with us, but so, too, will goodness. Children need to know this, believe it, and act upon it. Otherwise we are all in trouble."[28]

HELP CHILDREN SEE THE COMMONALITIES BETWEEN THEMSELVES AND OTHERS

In his comprehensive review of research conducted on children and empathy,[29] Dr. Mark Barnett concluded that children respond more empathetically to people whom they perceive as being similar in some way to themselves than they do to people they regard as being different. He suggests that parents who want to enhance their children's capacity for empathy should encourage children to see the similarities we all share as human beings. He cites the research of Martin Hoffman, which contends that children should be encouraged to participate in a wide range of experiences and interact with a diverse group of people.

"[A] child's perception of similarity to others," Barnett writes, "might also be promoted through the encouragement of universalistic beliefs and values that emphasize the connectedness of all people."[30] This hypothesis has been borne out by the Oliners' study on the altruistic personality. The Oliners discovered that the Christians who had rescued Jews during the height of the Holocaust were far more likely to have come from homes that practiced an inclusive, tolerant form of religion than were nonrescuers, whose religious backgrounds tended to be less inclusive and more focused on strict obedience to religious doctrine.

Dr. Grollman, who regularly talks with children of all religions about spiritual and psychological issues, has become increasingly concerned about what he sees as the growing tendency of people to be less inclusive and to focus their primary concerns and compassion on those who are part of their own particular group. "In theology," he explains, "there are two terms, particularism and universalism. More and more, I see religion moving toward particularism (What is good for my particular group?) as opposed to universalism (What is good for the community, or the world as a whole?). People are becoming more inbred. They are more often feeling, 'God is what my group says God is. If you disagree with us, you cannot find God.'

"Many people are focusing on individual salvation these days rather than on universal concerns. So people think if you're a rabbi and go to Oklahoma City, you go on behalf of the Jews. If you're a priest you go on behalf of the Catholics, and so on. We forget that there is one world and a universal God who created us all. I'll give you an example of what I mean. When I was asked to go to Oklahoma City, I made immediate travel plans and placed a call to a good friend of mine, another clergyman, to cancel a speaking engagement the following night at his church. He was very supportive and understanding of my need to go to the bombing site, but also a little surprised.

"'Gee, Earl, I didn't know there was much of a Jewish community out there,' he said.

"Frankly, I was a bit startled by the remark. 'Son-of-a-bitch,' I shot back. 'Who knows if anyone is Jewish or not? What does it matter? The explosion killed *people*. I'm less interested in their religion or their color than the fact that they're hurting. I belong in Oklahoma, even if there isn't a single Jew in the bunch.'

"My friend was silent for a moment, and then said ruefully, 'You're right, Earl. I *am* a son-of-a-bitch. And I want you to tell people that. Because it's a perfect example of the kind of mind-set we all seem to be falling into these days.'

"You see," Dr. Grollman explains, "when I sat and listened, hour after hour, day after day, to the pain and heartbreak of those families in Oklahoma City, when I hugged them and took them in my arms and felt their tears, being there was all that mattered. Not their religion or my religion; not their color or my color. We have to start putting the emphasis more on each other, and less on ourselves and the people who seem just like us because of their race or their religion.

"The beauty of the rainbow is caused by the variety of the colors. We are forgetting this, and it sends a dangerous message to our children. Because unless they lead extremely insular lives, many of the people they will meet and work with and need to depend upon will not be exactly like them."[31]

Ginny and Brian Klaus* agreed with Dr. Grollman's philosophy and decided to take some action. They entered their seven-year-old son, Jody, in an after-school arts program in a neighboring town.

"But there's a perfectly fine arts program just four

*pseudonyms

blocks away," Ginny Klaus's friend Anne pointed out. "What gives?"

"There's barely a half-dozen kids in this neighborhood that aren't white and Christian," Ginny answered. "I want Jody to be exposed to kids who aren't just like him. There's a whole big world out there, and he has to understand that there are other kids who don't look like him or worship like him or who may not have a nice big house."

"Ginny, he's only seven years old," said Anne. "He's used to the rec center here in town, and the kind of kids he's always known. Did you ever think that suddenly *he's* going to be the different one? Just so you can prove some kind of principle? He'll probably be more comfortable staying where he is."

"Well, maybe that's just the reason he should go," Ginny answered stubbornly.

But Ginny was less sure about her decision later that night. Thinking about what Anne had said, she confessed her doubts to her husband.

"Of course Jody'll find things in common with those kids," her husband replied. "They're not a different species—they're all a bunch of seven-year-olds."

Ginny nodded. Her husband seemed to be making sense. Despite her misgivings, she went ahead with her plans.

Three years later, she spoke about that decision at a parent workshop. "It was kind of prophetic, in a way. A little over a year later, the neighborhood started changing. It was clear that it wasn't going to stay as 'lily white' as it had been. We were getting African-Americans and Asians, with a few Arabs thrown in. These were all middle-class, professional people, but the neighborhood was different than it had been. Some of my neighbors found the adjustment hard going. But Jody took it in his stride. When the school scrambled to put together a special program to encourage kids to appreciate cultural diversity, Jody didn't understand what the big deal was. 'They're just kids, Mom,' he told me."

EMPHASIZE CHILDREN'S POWER TO POSITIVELY AFFECT OTHERS' LIVES

Interestingly, research shows that parents are far more likely to speak to their children about the consequences of their negative behavior than they are about the consequences of their positive behavior.[32] This is understandable. We have become a society that frequently focuses on the negative. Also, children's negative behavior is often socially and academically disruptive and can be embarrassing for their parents.

In contrast, positive actions taken by children are often quieter and less dramatic. Parents are less motivated to discuss the consequences of positive actions. Aren't they, after all, fairly self-evident, especially to the children themselves?

Not necessarily, many researchers contend. "The research supports the importance of pointing out to children the consequences of their positive behavior, particularly how they have the ability to help others," says Dr. Staub. "When parents do this, children are able to enter another's world. It's what leads to empathy and compassion and is a very important piece of guidance. Helping children learn to take the role of the other enables them to understand their own potential power to affect people's welfare in a positive or negative way."[33]

After the bombing in Oklahoma City, thousands of young people sent letters, drawings, food, and money, and prayed for the victims in their houses of worship. Pointing out to children how such gestures of kindness affect others is very important.

Dr. Grollman, recalling his days in Oklahoma City, speaks of embracing an elderly African-American woman as she wept and told him, "I'm thanking God for one thing that happened here."

"You mean there was some sign that your grandchild might be alive?" he exclaimed.

"No," she said, shaking her head. "Not that. I'm starting to realize I'll probably never see him again. But for the first time ever, people cared and tried to help me. And they didn't give a damn what color I am. No one can know how that makes me feel."[34]

DON'T STEREOTYPE GIRLS' AND BOYS' CAPACITY FOR EMPATHY

Over the years, numerous research studies have linked gender to the capacity for empathy.[35] Generally, such studies concluded that the mother was the most important parent in determining whether children grew into kind, caring, compassionate human beings. Many of these studies also concluded that girls tended to be more empathetic than boys, although one researcher contended that boys could be as compassionate as girls if they had experienced certain family problems, which presumably made them more sensitized to the pain of others.[36]

Lately, however, these findings have been re-evaluated in the light of important new research data. As a result, long-standing stereotypes are starting to erode. A 26-year longitudinal study that tracked 70 children from approximately five years of age through adulthood found that one of the most important factors that seemed to determine the subjects' capacity for empathy was the amount of time they had spent with their fathers.[37] Dr. Richard Koester, the lead investigator in the study, speculated in a *New York Times* interview that the more time a father spent with his children, the more sensitized he became to his children's needs, which led him to act more empathetically toward them. "'And it may be,' he said, 'that those fathers who are more willing to spend that much time with their children are more empathic [to begin with].'"[38]

The previous dearth of reliable data about the father's role in the development of empathy in children had contributed in part to the traditional emphasis on the mother's role in this process, particularly to the belief that empathic mothers tended to produce empathic sons. Interestingly, the degree of empathy evidenced by girls was viewed as less dependent on their mothers' characteristics. Girls were seen as being more "naturally" predisposed toward this trait, regardless of their mothers'—or fathers'—actions. They did not seem to be in need of an "extra boost" in the way some researchers thought boys might be.

Dr. Eisenberg cautions that we actually know little about the influence of fathers on the development—or lack of development—of empathy in their children, because relatively few fathers have participated in formal research studies. "It's been very difficult to obtain their involvement," she says. "It's like pulling teeth. Since mothers, in the past, were more available and more willing to be studied, much of the theory about parental involvement in children's characterological and spiritual development has been focused on them. But this does not necessarily mean that fathers have less of an impact in this area than mothers do."[39] In fact, studies such as Dr. Koester's offer concrete evidence that fathers' actions are very much a part of the equation.

Dr. Eisenberg also questions past research findings that support the widespread belief that females tend to be more empathic than males. "Are females really warmer and more nurturing than men? Well, the research varies greatly, depending upon the methods researchers use to measure this phenomenon," she points out. "For example, when researchers use self-reporting measures, females come out way ahead. But when researchers utilize more objective measures, such as subtle facial expressions, there's either no difference or very weak differences. What I would say is that females *think* they are more empathic than males. And that belief colors the way they regard their own behavior, as well as the way others regard their behavior. It is also true that girls tend to value helpfulness as a trait more than boys do. So when a boy engages in a kind, helpful act, he may not define it as such. Girls, on the other hand, are more likely to do so.

"The bottom line is that parents and other caring adults need to be cautious in making assumptions about children's capacity for empathy based on their sex. Don't assume anything. Treat each child as having the same potential, despite what the child might say."[40]

EXPLICITLY CONDEMN ACTS OF HATRED AND VIOLENCE TO YOUR CHILDREN

The research indicates that when parents and other adults fail to explicitly condemn acts of hatred and violence, children tend to misinterpret this silence as tacit acceptance or indifference.[41]

Dr. Staub, who has extensively researched the crucial role that bystanders play in either helping to prevent or tacitly encouraging acts of hatred and violence, warns that the actions of bystanders have a crucial impact on children. "When evil acts are not explicitly condemned by parents and other adults, this can be misinterpreted by children in a number of ways," he says. "Children may assume that their parents agree with these acts or do not think such acts are morally wrong or, even more troubling, they might come to the conclusion that this is simply the way people operate, and that evil and a lack of resistance to evil is the norm in this world.

"Certainly not every parent is inclined to be a public activist when evil occurs. There are many reasons for this: lack of time, lack of resources, or a genuine concern for their children's safety. Parents may feel that if they strongly condemn certain acts, their children might take action at some future time and put themselves in physical or emotional jeopardy.

"But the danger of silence is, in my opinion, much greater than the danger of speech. Children often draw negative interpretations from parents' silence and/or inaction. They may see their parents as hypocrites, or as cowards. This is not only harmful for children's moral development but can affect their ability to trust and respect their mothers and fathers."[42]

Dr. Staub's research suggests that parents should not be reluctant to explain to their children the reasons for their actions or inaction. "It is tremendously valuable for children when parents fully explain their concerns about evil acts on the one hand and their concerns about possible danger on the other hand," he emphasizes. "They can discuss their conflicts and explore with their children other ways—besides public actions—in which evil can be thwarted. For instance, they can support groups that are taking a public stand, or show by their own example how they think people should be treated."[43]

In Billings, Montana, in 1993, skinheads and neo-Nazis began a campaign of hate and harassment against Hispanics, African-Americans, Jews, and other minorities. The vast majority of Billings residents were repelled by what was happening in the town. Religious and community leaders proposed that people take a dramatic stand against the hate groups, but action involved a clear element of risk.

Citizens had to search their consciences and consider the possible consequences. While thousands of residents participated in acts of dramatic resistance (described in detail in Chapter Four), others chose not to, although they were good people and deplored the racism and anti-Semitism perpetrated by the actions of a few. Their reasons ranged from concern for their children's safety and concern about vandalism and escalated violence to a genuine conviction that there were quieter and less dramatic ways for people to combat hate crimes.

Some of these adults, who were parents, then had to explain to their children why they were not joining their neighbors in public acts of protest. I listened to the explanations of several of these people and was struck by their honesty in dealing with their children. Each made an effort to ensure that their children understood in no uncertain terms that they did not agree with the actions of the haters. They spoke strongly about their opposition to harassment and persecution because of skin color or religion or beliefs, and openly discussed their safety concerns. They also discussed other actions they were taking that were more private but would, they felt, also be of help. These included providing financial support to the Billings Coalition of Human Rights, keeping a watchful eye on neighbors who might be at risk, and immediately calling the police when they suspected any hint of trouble. Many of these parents were also working within their churches and other community groups to improve understanding and communication between people of different races and religious beliefs. As a result of their careful explanations, their children understood that their parents' public inaction did not constitute approval of or indifference to hate crimes.

The role of the bystander is often seen as a moral barometer of society. History shows that when evil acts occur and good people stand by without taking action, those acts tend to progress. In these cases, Dr. Staub points out, the bystanders as well as the victims suffer:

"When people do not take a stand against evil, they become diminished. There is a part of them that knows they should be doing something, and when they do not there is a certain amount of guilt, and a certain need to rationalize their behavior, which often involves distancing themselves from the victims. When this occurs, it is the perpetrators who benefit."[44]

Interestingly, the bystander phenomenon appears to intrigue the general population as well as social scientists. Miles Lerman, chairman of the United States Holocaust Memorial Council and one of the creators of the United States Holocaust Memorial Museum in Washington, D.C., commented in a recent interview in *The New York Times* on the interest that museum visitors often express about this topic: "'We had no idea that people would be fascinated by the role of the bystander, the presumably good person who found it convenient to look the other way in the face of horror and evil [during the Holocaust]. Our visitors question that again and again, and we now see that part of our mission is to encourage discussion about moral responsibility, to get people talking about what it means to be human and to make choices.'"[45]

Such discussions need not take place only in national museums. When they occur in the home, between parent and child, the impact is even more powerful.

Chapter Two
HELPING CHILDREN COPE WITH PRIME-TIME VIOLENCE

Children today are exposed to violence in a number of ways. They may witness violence between others in their homes, schools, and neighborhoods. They may be victims of violence, or they may hear about acts of violence. Each of these happenings has consequences for children, based upon the severity of each situation and a child's particular vulnerability. But for most youngsters, the media, particularly television, is the greatest source of exposure to violence and bloodshed.

It is estimated that the average American child watches approximately 25 hours of television a week. The research findings of one prominent investigator, Dr. George Gerbner, indicate that "over the last two decades the three major networks have averaged about five acts of violence an hour in their prime-time schedule . . . . On Saturday morning, when most children do most of their viewing, the networks averaged about 25 acts of violence an hour for the last 15 years."[1] Other research findings, with somewhat different numbers, back up Dr. Gerbner's assessment of the preponderance of television violence.[2]

HOW CHILDREN ARE AFFECTED BY TV VIOLENCE

How does constant exposure to the violence shown on television affect children? Each child is unique and has his own response, but researchers have found that repeatedly viewing television violence often causes children to experience anxiety and show increased aggressive behavior.

Increased anxiety

Dr. Gerbner, who has studied the effect of television violence on children for more than 20 years, has found that heavy television viewers tend to see the world as being more violent, and express more fear and anxiety about their environment, than do less frequent viewers.[3] Findings from other research studies bear this out.[4] Gerbner calls this phenomenon the "mean-world syndrome" and explains that "the more we are exposed to violence-laden television, the more we . . . absorb a sense of mistrust and insecurity, a sense of living in a mean and dangerous world."[5]

Increased aggressive behavior

Almost 30 years ago, when the *Batman* television series was at its height, I noticed a rash of little boys dressed up as perfect Batman miniatures. Armed with appropriate arsenals, they seemed to be everywhere at the after-school program where I worked. The little girls were for the most part forlornly left out of the fun, except for the few enterprising ones who came dressed as miniature Batgirls.

One could easily have sat back and enjoyed the involvement of the children, had not a very interesting phenomenon occurred. The character of Batman was taken so thoroughly to heart that not only were boys dressed like him, they also started acting like him, which meant that some unfortunate children not in costume were delegated to be Batman's archenemies. My supervisors and I made several impromptu surveys and found out that "child crime" at the after-school program (consisting mostly of pulled hair, punched noses, and snatched finger paints) had definitely increased during this period.

Fast-forward to 1995 and replace Batman with The Power Rangers™. Not much has changed except that some might say progress has been made because little girls are now just as involved in dressing up and imitating violent all-powerful heroes as are little boys: Both sexes find it hard to resist the seductive allure of mythic figures who fight for good but use violence in order to triumph.

A number of research studies have concluded that when children are consistently exposed to television violence, they show increased aggression.[6] That can mean more aggressive physical behavior, such as shoving and kicking, or more aggressive social behavior, such as threats and intimidation. After all, if a television "hero" uses violence to reach his goal or to thwart the actions of the "bad guys," why then would children feel they need to reject this kind of behavior? In fact, research shows that media villains actually kill fewer people than do the good guys.

During the past dozen years, I've led more than 100 classroom discussions with children that focused on the concept of heroism. In these discussions, students from kindergarten through third grade were asked to give their definition of a hero. Most children (though not all) spoke of superheroes on TV. Physical strength and an ability to attack and demolish the villains were attributes that were greatly admired.

"But why is it so important to be physically strong?" I asked. "Aren't there other ways to deal with bullies?" A second grader, looking at me with a mixture of pity and scorn, replied, "Don't you know what goes on out there?"

HELPING CHILDREN COPE

Although our world is dangerous and sometimes unjust, Dr. Gerbner's ongoing research indicates that this bleak view is so exaggerated for children, who largely form their view of the world from television, that it distorts the reality.

What can parents and teachers do to help counter this distortion? Happily, they can do a number of things.

Open Up a Dialogue with Children

In my experience, parents of children who live in relatively safe neighborhoods are often not aware of their children's concerns about violence because children tend not to articulate these anxieties. A second or third or fourth grader will not tell a parent, "Mom, I've been feeling a lot of anxiety about the level of violence in our society" or "Dad, I'm concerned about my safety in a world that seems very scary. What, exactly, is being done to protect me?"

Adults must sometimes gently and sensitively initiate the subject of violence themselves and begin a dialogue with children about the violence they see and hear around them. For example, while parents cannot always control what their children see on television, they *can* make an effort to watch and discuss selected shows with them. When violent scenes arise, they can encourage youngsters to think about ways in which people (and cartoon characters) can solve problems without hurting and killing one another. They can emphasize that we all have choices regarding how we react to the difficulties that confront us, and that with each choice comes different consequences and responsibilities—a concept that is rarely explored in movies and television shows.

Emphasize to Children Ways They Are Protected

Talk to your children about concrete actions being taken to help protect them. These might include burglar alarms in your home, police patrols guarding the neighborhood, and community watch groups that encourage neighbors to look out for one another.

Also remind children of what they themselves can do to increase their own safety, such as remembering their address and phone number and not talking to strangers or wandering off by themselves in public places.

Each child's needs and emotional makeup are different, so take your cues from your child regarding just how much specific information she needs and wants to hear. Remember that what is comforting to one child may provoke discomfort and anxiety in another.

Talk with Children about What They Can Do to Feel Better

When children are feeling anxious and frightened:
- They can talk about their feelings.
- They can discuss with adults what they can do to help them be safer.
- They can use their imaginations to create drawings, tell stories, and act out situations similar to what's upsetting them, in which they choose the endings and how the characters react. This helps children feel more powerful and in control.

When children are feeling sad:
- They can cry if they want to.
- They can reach out to help others who might be feeling sad.
- They can remember happy times they have spent with their family and friends.

When they are feeling angry:
- They can vent their anger in ways that are allowed in the household. For example, they can punch a punching bag as hard as they can.

Whatever the particular feelings children experience, encouraging them to communicate their emotions to the people who are close to them provides an important outlet. Keep in mind that not every child will want or be able to use words to communicate. Drawing a picture or communicating by a touch or a look can be just as effective if children feel they are being treated with warmth and respect.

WATCHING THE TRIAL OF THE CENTURY

For almost a year, televised images, analyses, and discussion about the O.J. Simpson murder trial permeated the media. While this was happening, our nation's children were watching and listening. What were they thinking? And what did the "trial of the century" teach them?

In April of 1995, a series of discussions took place with approximately 200 children from grades four through seven, focusing on their reactions to the O.J. Simpson trial and related issues. Three New Jersey public schools participated. One was located in an inner-city, one in an affluent professional community, and one in a predominantly middle-class neighborhood. Eight classes of approximately 25 children each were involved. The discussions were conducted by a guidance counselor, a school social worker, and a clinical social worker and state judge who worked as a team. All of the classes were asked the same four questions:

1) Are you aware of what's been happening in the

O.J. Simpson trial?

2) Do you feel that O.J. Simpson is getting a fair trial, and why?

3) What are your definitions of the terms "justice" and "a fair trial"?

4) Do you think most people in our country receive a fair trial?

This was not a scientific study. Rather, it was a series of conversations designed to get a sense of what these young people were thinking. Those of us who were involved in the project had initially thought that children's perceptions would be largely influenced by their race, the socioeconomic group they belonged to, and where they lived. But we were surprised to discover that the vast majority of children we spoke to had come to almost identical conclusions (though not always for the same reasons) regarding the trial, as well as more general issues of justice and fairness in our country's legal system. We found those conclusions troubling both for the children as individuals and for society as a whole. But . . . let the children speak for themselves.

Are you aware of what's been happening in the O.J. Simpson trial?

At the time we talked with them, virtually all of the children—no matter what their race, background, or geographic location might be—told us that they were following the trial and knew what was taking place. They all reported getting their information from the same sources: television, radio, newspapers (a few children specified the *National Inquirer* and *Star* magazine), and from listening to adult conversations. When we asked if the children's parents or teachers had talked with them about the case to help explain what was happening or answer any questions they might have about the trial, almost none of the children answered "yes."

During the discussions, the vast majority of the children were able to recite the basic facts of the trial, although not without some confusion and distortion. For example, a fourth grader explained to the discussion leader that O.J. Simpson played football. "And what did he do after being a football star?" the child was asked. "Kill people," he answered authoritatively.

Do you feel that O.J. Simpson is getting a fair trial, and why?

Virtually every child expressed his opinion that O.J. Simpson was not getting a fair trial. Following is a representative sampling of their reasons.

A number of children thought O.J. Simpson would not get a fair trial because he's a celebrity.

> O.J. Simpson can play football better than other people so now he's getting special treatment.
> (a fourth grader)

I don't think he'll get a fair trial. I think he'll get treated real, real good because he was a football star.
(a fifth grader)

I think that with the O.J. Simpson trial, just like all the other famous people trials, he's getting special treatment because he's famous. If it were you or I, we'd just be treated like dirt.
(a fifth grader)

I think he's just gonna walk. I think the jury won't be able to decide whether he's guilty or innocent because everybody knows who he is and likes him from when he played football and stuff.
(a sixth grader)

He's so wealthy and everyone likes O.J. because he's a superstar, and he has a lot of money. So he can keep the trial going to make sure he wins.
(a sixth grader)

Here you have a person who's, like, a Heisman trophy winner; a role model to other people. You're not gonna get a fair trial with a person like that.
(a seventh grader)

Other children thought he would not be treated fairly because of racial issues.

He won't get a fair trial. It's getting to be all about race. And there was this radio show where a guy faked a

Japanese accent to make fun of Judge Ito.
(a fourth grader)

I don't think he'll get a fair trial, especially with a jury where there isn't one white male.
(a fifth grader)

A lot of people are prejudiced, you know.
(a fifth grader)

He won't get a fair trial because the jury is just being racist to each other.
(a fifth grader)

The defense keeps trying to bring up [things] like race . . . . It shouldn't be in this trial because it doesn't make much sense.
(a sixth grader)

It isn't fair because one of the police officers who found some of the evidence, they say he's a racist and he admitted that he's a racist.
(a sixth grader)

If the jury is the same race maybe they might say he's innocent just because they're the same type of people. I think they should try to get all different kinds of people on the jury.
(a sixth grader)

It's not fair because the defense is going on mostly about race. That's mostly what they are talking about.
(a seventh grader)

Many children brought up the role of the media when they said Simpson would not get a fair trial.

> I think the media has stooped way too low.
> (a fourth grader)

> I think it's getting out of hand . . . . They're publishing it and putting it on television. It's on all the trash shows like *Hard Copy*, and they're saying all these lies. Well, I think they're lies.
> (a fifth grader)

> A whole lot of newspapers are making this like a comic strip.
> (a fifth grader)

> It's in all the newspapers and everything . . . . I think the only way he could get a fair trial is if they got a jury from a foreign country that could speak English but wouldn't know anything about it.
> (a sixth grader)

Some children said Simpson would not get a fair trial because of problems with the jury.

> Some of the jurors, they just seem kind of weird.
> (a fifth grader)

> I think the reason we all think O.J. Simpson can't get a fair trial is because we're giving the jury too much power . . . . They're rebelling against everybody. We shouldn't give them that much power. We should just tell them to do their

duties and tell the truth.
(a sixth grader)

I think you should pick jurors with college degrees or something. Because if you pick, like, a really stupid juror who doesn't know anything about courts, they're not going to do anything to help the trial. So I think you should pick people who are smart.
(a sixth grader)

How can he get a fair trial when the jurors are all getting dismissed?
(a seventh grader)

Children gave other reasons why the trial was not a fair one.

There's a lot of things going on, like suspicion that people planted stuff.
(a fourth grader)

He has a lot of lawyers, and they are getting him out of situations.
(a fourth grader)

They don't have everything in control, and the lawyers keep screaming at each other.
(a fifth grader)

It's very confusing. There are so many things that, like, prove him guilty and other things that, like, prove him

innocent . . . . A lot of it feels like a set-up.
(a fifth grader)

They don't have enough evidence, but [everyone's] already made their mind up anyway.
(a fifth grader)

They're trying to frame him.
(a sixth grader)

A lot of people are treating O.J. unfairly, and focusing on things like Marcia Clark's new haircut.
(a sixth grader)

People are accusing him of murder without hearing the defense side.
(a seventh grader)

Life isn't fair.
(a seventh grader)

Virtually none of the children told us they thought the trial was fair, but a few of them did express uncertainty. One fourth grader talked about her confusion and then offered her idea for another way of proceeding.

"Why don't they just let O.J. speak for himself?" she said. "The judge would say, 'Did you do it, O.J.?' And he'd say 'yes' or 'no.' If he says 'yes,' he goes to jail. If he says 'no,' he goes free. He has to be honest, though."

It should be noted that children of all ages at each school were generally quite critical of the jurors and the lawyers. They tended, however, to have a more positive assessment of Judge Ito. Some children thought they might aspire to be a judge, though none of them spoke of wanting to be a juror or a lawyer. Being a judge, one sixth grader pointed out, had certain advantages. "If I had to choose between being a judge or a lawyer, I'd rather be a judge, because I'd get to throw people out of courtrooms and stuff. There's the fun in that one."

What are your definitions of the terms "justice" and "a fair trial"?

A majority of the children seemed to have a basic understanding of the concept of justice. For example:

> Justice is when they don't send you to jail for something you didn't do.
> (a fourth grader)

> Justice is what's true and fair and right.
> (a fifth grader)

> Justice is when every bad guy that ever did something wrong gets the proper punishment.
> (a sixth grader)

> Justice is when you get your chance to prove you are innocent, and you get to hire a lawyer.
> (a seventh grader)

But many of the children we spoke with were not so sure

that every person deserved justice. If a crime was terrible enough, perhaps not, they seemed to feel. By coincidence, these discussions took place shortly after the bombing in Oklahoma City. The majority of children in all grades and in every school thought that the bomber would not and should not get a fair trial.

In one fifth-grade class, the discussion leader asked, "Do you think the Oklahoma City bomber will be able to get a fair trial?"

"No!" the class answered in unison.

"Why?"

"Because he did a very bad thing," one child answered.

"Because he shouldn't get off," said another.

"But even though he's accused of doing a bad thing," the children were asked, "do you agree that he deserves a trial?"

"Yeah!" (in unison)

"But not a fair trial?"

"Yeah!" (in unison)

A sixth grader talking about Timothy McVeigh, the accused bomber, told us: "A man who goes out and kills 150 people and children, he won't get a fair trial. Just the way he attacked the Federal Building itself; never mind going out and doing it to any old building. He's going after the government. And without [the government], we're all in trouble."

Another sixth grader, echoing the sentiments of many of the children, stated emphatically, "He's not going to get a fair trial because [he] killed all those babies and stuff."

Do you think most people in our country receive a fair trial?

I think everybody in America gets a fair trial because that's kind of like the law.
(a fourth grader)

No, because people sometimes, just for no reason, they put [other people] in jail without proof.
(a fourth grader)

I think it depends on who the person is, because if the person is black, there'll be racism.
(a fourth grader)

No, because most people are innocent, and they get accused of things they didn't do.
(a fifth grader)

Most trials aren't fair . . . they don't try to look at your good side. They try and find all the bad parts.
(a fifth grader)

It depends. Not if someone, like, flees the state like O.J. Simpson did. Or if they blow up a building or something, like in Oklahoma.
(a sixth grader)

I think everybody in America does definitely get a fair trial, maybe even too fair a trial . . . we need a lot [of evidence] compared to some other countries.
(a sixth grader)

Most people who are famous don't get a fair trail, because everyone pretty much suspects that person.
(a seventh grader)

It depends on the jury and the judge.
(a seventh grader)

Two of the children who participated in these discussions spoke of relatives who had been sent to jail after a trial. For this reason, they said, they knew that people didn't get a fair trial. Their definition of "fair," however, was far from objective.

"I know people don't get fair trials," a fourth grader forcefully told the class, "because my uncle got put in jail. There was this guy in Florida, where my uncle was, and he was in a bar and started a fight with the bartender, and my uncle yelled, 'Stop, stop, stop!' Then my uncle hit him and then the man got a bat and broke my uncle's [car] window and then my uncle beat him up with the baseball bat and then my uncle went to trial and was found guilty."

A fifth grader told us, "They said my stepfather robbed someone. He said he didn't, but they put him in jail anyway just because they had evidence."

Countering Children's Cynicism

Why is it that virtually every child we spoke with expressed a deep cynicism about the criminal-justice system and repeatedly stated the belief that most people in this country cannot expect to get a fair trial? Is it because of sensationalism and distortion in the media regarding high-profile celebrity cases such as O.J. Simpson's? Or is it because parents and other caring adults are not taking the time to talk with children about their questions, thoughts, and misconceptions about high-profile trials and other events reported in the media?

What can parents, teachers, and other adults do to help children understand the purpose and goals of the American system of justice and view high-profile trials in a more balanced way? The following guidelines come from educators, mental-health professionals, attorneys, and judges:

- Talk with children about high-profile cases they see and hear in the media.
- Ask children what they are thinking and feeling. Never assume you know what's on their minds. Not all children will be able to give direct answers, but many will. This will help you get a sense of what may be troubling or confusing them.
- Answer children's questions as best you can. If there are some questions that stump you, the research librarian in your local library may be able to help you find some answers.
- Educate children about some of the basic concepts of our country's system of justice and some of the values that we as a people believe in. For example, our legal system embraces the following: A person is innocent until proven guilty; jurors from all walks of life are expected to serve on juries; most jurors are not sequestered; *all* jurors are expected to tell

the truth and be guided by the truth.

- Begin a continuing dialogue with children about the meaning of justice. Ask them for their definition of justice, and whether they think there is justice in the courts or in their own lives. Encourage them to be specific and give examples from what happens in school, with their friends, and in their family. If they seem to believe justice is sometimes—or often—lacking, talk with them about what they can do to change this in their own lives.

- Encourage children to think about what would be a fair punishment for someone who breaks a rule or acts in a way that's hurtful or destructive to others. Ask them to give reasons for their conclusions.

- Most important, remember that children often form their ideas about justice on the basis of what they think their parents believe. Be very aware of what you convey to children by your general attitudes and your remarks and conversations with other adults (which children may or may not overhear).

I frequently ask children when they've broken the rules or misbehaved in some way what they think would be a fair punishment. Often they are very hard on themselves.

"Don't feed me for a *week*," an eight-year-old told me.

"Make me stay in my room with all the blinds pulled down, *forever*," a five-year-old suggested.

"I'll do all the cooking and cleaning," said a six-year-old who had never done either.

"Don't give me my allowance for a month," a seven-year-old said firmly. Then, after a pause, "But could you give me money for my mom's birthday present?"

The concept of punishment fitting the crime is a sophisticated one, and not easily understood by young children. It's helpful to initiate talks with your children about the concept of fairness.

When six-year-old Timothy* accidentally breaks a glass bowl with his ball, he is expected to help pay for the bowl's repair because he knew that he was not allowed to play ball indoors. He receives no other punishment. This prompts his eight-year-old brother, Max, to protest. Max was punished earlier that week for telling a willful lie and specifically disobeying his father; his punishment was to come straight home from school for several days and to complete several extra chores.

"It's not fair!" he says, contending that Timothy should get the same punishment that he did.

Instead of punishing Max for his defiance, his parents explain to him that some misbehaviors are more serious than others, and that more serious misbehaviors require stronger punishments. For example, lying is serious, as is hurting someone or destroying property. But staying up past one's bedtime, throwing away or trading one's lunch, and not brushing one's teeth are less serious.

Parents can also use reasoning to help children understand the important concept of making restitution. When they've done something wrong and hurt people's feelings, disappointed people, or destroyed property, ask them to suggest ways to make up for what they have done. Children are often very creative in this regard. If she has

* pseudonym

no ideas or her ideas are not appropriate, tell her what you have decided she should do to try to make restitution, and why she's being asked to do it. She may not agree with your idea of justice, but she will get a sense that people should at least attempt to seek and obtain it.

Note: At this writing, several months had passed since the O.J. Simpson trial ended. While our team did not go back into the classrooms to discuss children's reactions to the verdict, we did speak to a number of youngsters individually and informally.

Not surprisingly, many children expressed even more cynicism than they had earlier. Unlike in our previous discussions with the children, this time opinions were divided almost solely along racial lines, reflecting adult reactions across the country. The children appeared to share one overriding belief: Justice had not been served.

The white children (even some of those who had previously expressed doubts about Simpson's guilt) now declared that he should have been found guilty. And African-American children, approving of the verdict, expressed anger that so many white people were upset that Simpson had not been convicted. "They're just acting that way because he's black," a seven-year-old told me.

Interestingly, when I asked children (as I had the previous spring) if their parents had discussed or explained the verdict to them, they told me no, although they were very aware of their parents' reactions and had overheard adults talk about the trial.

"He's [O.J. Simpson] just laughing at us, because he got away with murder," a nine-year-old assured me.

"How do you know that?" I asked him.

"I just know," he told me positively.

"But how?" I persisted.

"Because that's what my mom told my aunt," he explained.

TALKING WITH CHILDREN ABOUT WAR

During the period our country was at war in the Persian Gulf, I was asked to advise schools and community groups about how to help children cope with the psychological impact of the conflict. In this capacity, I was repeatedly struck by some of the lessons children were learning (and not learning) from this experience.

Children whose parents were serving in the military were understandably deeply distressed. However, the majority of other children apparently took the war in stride, despite the predictable anxieties they experienced. This may have been due in large part to the sensitivity accorded children's psychological needs by many adults, including some well-known media figures. However, a number of youngsters seemed to regard the war as just one more example of the violence that turns up daily on their televisions and, for some, on their street corners.

Without understanding the complexities involved, many children felt that the country went to war primarily to "kick Saddam Hussein's ass," a phrase repeated again and again by young boys echoing the words of President Bush.

Children were convinced that we could win the conflict because our country was bigger and stronger than Iraq, and because our soldiers and bombs were smarter than theirs. "They'll never beat us," one fourth grader assured me. "We have all the computers and stuff."

Many children did not tend to think about the war's cost in terms of human life or suffering. Though numerous class projects were designed at this time to cheer and support our troops, there was less focus on the ethical and moral implications of war, especially in the younger grades. In my talks with children, youngsters showed relatively little understanding or conviction that war should be a last resort, and that human life, even that of the Iraqi "bad guys," is precious.

Children's concerns, understandably, were focused on how they personally would be affected by the war. A first grader asked me, "Somebody said that Saddam Hussein has missiles that can travel all the way over here. He doesn't, does he?" A third grader said, "Saddam is going to send poison gas to the United States, and we'll all have to wear gas masks, like in Israel." A fourth grader worried that Hussein would cut off our oil supply. "He wants to stop us from getting any oil, so people won't be able to drive their cars. But, then, how would I get to soccer practice?"

Of course, there was great relief that the war was swift and decisive and that so few Americans died. Young and old were spared the lurid images of death and destruction we had feared might be broadcast nightly from the front. As it turned out, almost all the death and devastation were sustained by Iraqis and rarely appeared on television. So children saw very little of the terror and true nature of warfare. Instead, their view of the war was dominated by vivid images of high-tech missiles arcing through the sky and detonating targets in a crimson flash. As many observers have noted, it was like the ultimate Nintendo game. Children's imaginations were captured by the shiny "smart" weaponry, which seemed to dwarf any concerns about human consequences when those weapons hit their marks.

In many children's minds, the Persian Gulf War seemed to sanction the use of violence to resolve disagreements and promoted war as an acceptable, if not superior, way of dealing with an international bully.

Fostering Respect for Life

It's important that, as a society, we look at what our values communicate to our children. Along with imbuing our children with patriotism, should we not also nurture respect for human life? To help convey this message, mental-health experts suggest:

- When military conflicts occur, specifically emphasize to children that war and fighting should always be a last resort.
- Talk to children about the things that can be done— and are being done—to try to resolve conflicts peacefully in the schools and at home. Explain that employees and employers can go to specially trained people to help them settle disputes. Talk

about the role of diplomacy, and of the United Nations, in trying to help countries end conflicts and wars. Explain the role our own country has played in helping to bring peace to the Middle East and in trying to end the bloodshed in Bosnia. Emphasize to children that although there are conflicts and warfare in this world, there are also many people working individually and within groups to stop the violence.

- Let children know that you believe there is too much violence in this world, and that it is up to all of us to find ways to cut down on this violence.
- Ask children for their ideas on how we can do this. Some of the suggestions from children I have talked with include holding your temper, not jumping to conclusions, giving the person you're mad at a chance to explain, and "no hitting!"
- Brainstorm with children about ways to help the victims of war. For example, children might donate part of their allowance, or be involved in fund-raising drives to provide food or needed medical supplies.
- Let children know that they can contribute (even in small ways) to making the world a more peaceful place by their *own* behavior toward others.

Helping Children Control Their Own Behavior

During the worst of the fighting in the Bosnian conflict, I talked with a group of fourth graders about the war. All knew what was happening in Bosnia and, in contrast to their understanding of the Gulf War, children were very aware of the human cost of war because of the images of death and mutilation shown on the evening news. All the youngsters in the group were indignant and angry about the war. Although they were not fearful for themselves, they felt strongly for the children in Bosnia who were enduring war's cruelties.

"Why do they hate each other so much?" one girl asked.

I answered that these feelings had built up over a long time and had finally exploded into the violence the class had been seeing on their television sets. Then I asked the class what they would have done to prevent the war if they had been the leader of Bosnia before the hostilities erupted. Here are some of their answers:

"Have the people try to talk to each other."

"Have them try to understand each other's feelings."

"Tell everyone to try to compromise."

"Get another person who's fair to listen and try to solve the problem."

"Have everyone take time out."

We then talked about how angry words can escalate into pushing, shoving, hitting, or worse. I asked class members how they could use some of their good ideas in their own lives when they encountered bullies or felt angry and frustrated because they thought they weren't being treated fairly.

The children made several suggestions, including taking time to "cool off" and having somebody mediate during an argument. As with adults, children don't always follow their own advice. But thinking and talking about possible solutions can be an important first step in changing children's behavior and expectations—of both themselves and others.

Chapter Three
WHEN BAD THINGS HAPPEN CLOSE TO HOME

A long with being affected by the mayhem they see in cartoons, movies, and news of distant events, children must sometimes confront the existence of violence in their own world. A number of years ago, I conducted a research study about the impact of a young child's murder on his friends and classmates. This case was particularly tragic and upsetting because the child, a five-year-old boy, was killed by his seriously depressed mother, who also attempted to kill herself. By all accounts, the mother had been a loving and devoted parent before her illness, and many of the children in the neighborhood knew and liked her. She seemed, in fact, much like every other mother.

How could it be explained to these youngsters that a child, just like themselves, had not only died but had been killed by a parent? How would it affect them, and what actions could parents take that would strengthen these children's ability to cope?

CHILDREN REACT

The children's responses to Joshua's* death are common reactions experienced by children who confront sad and frightening events. Such reactions include:

Wanting to know the facts

Almost every child asked very specific facts. Jane, age five, wanted to know, "Which ledge of the building did Joshua land on? Where was Joshua? Where was Joshua's father? Where was Joshua's mother? Where was the window?"

Craig, age six and a half, asked, "How did Joshua look after he went out the window? Was there blood? Did his bones break? What happened to Joshua's body?"

Peter, age eight and a half, inquired of his mother several times, "How do you think he felt? Did he suffer? Was he in pain? Did Joshua cry? Did it hurt?"

Questions about Joshua's mother's motivation for killing her son were particularly frequent.

Steven, age six, kept repeating, "Was Joshua's mother really sick? She didn't look sick. Did anyone know she was sick?"

Martin, age six and a half, wanted to know, "How was

*The names of the victim and all the children in this study have been changed.

Joshua's mother sick? How can you be sick in the head? Was Joshua's father sick also?"

Patricia, age eight, spent much time speculating about Joshua's death and asked her mother, "Why did Joshua's mother do it? Had he been bad? Why didn't his mother die, too?" She finally concluded by herself that Joshua's mother was bigger, and Joshua's bones were more easily crushed.

The children's reasoning as to why Joshua's mother threw him out of the window were varied and sometimes unusually insightful.

Jane thought that "maybe Joshua's mother was so unhappy that she didn't want to live anymore and didn't want to be without her little boy."

Molly, age six and a half, was speculating with her parents about Joshua's mother and said, "Maybe she was so sick that no one believed her, and she did this so they'd believe her."

Patricia, when telling her mother what happened, explained that "Joshua's mother did what she did because she was very sick and had a lot of problems."

Larry, age eight, came to the conclusion that "if [Joshua's mother] wanted to die herself, maybe she wanted Joshua to die too, so she wouldn't be alone."

Anxiety

Predictably, many of the children felt and expressed great anxiety about the death.

Several days after Joshua's death, Andrew, age five, asked his mother plaintively when she became angry with him, "Will you throw me out the window?"

The day after Steven found out about Joshua's death,

he seemingly casually asked his mother, "Would you throw me out the window? Are you sick, too?"

Shortly after learning of Joshua's death, Heather suddenly insisted that her mother stay with her at night. Her mother felt that she was frightened of being abandoned. Whenever her mother tried to leave the room, Heather said, "If you loved me you'd stay with me. How will I know what you'll do when I'm sleeping? How do I know you won't leave?" She seemed very upset, and asked tremulously, "Would you ever throw me out the window?"

A week after Joshua's death, Molly went to her mother and said solemnly, "I have a question to ask. Would you ever do that to me?" Her mother reassured her, but days later, when her father asked, "Do you really think your Mommy or Daddy would throw you out the window?" she responded by saying thoughtfully, "Well, sometimes you can feel one way and act another."

Immediately after Peter heard about Joshua's death, he went to his mother and said he had heard that Joshua's mother had thrown him out the window because she was crazy. He then said to her, as if confiding a horrible and confusing secret, "I didn't say anything, Mom, but I know she *wasn't* crazy. I used to see her all the time, and she looked like all the other mothers!"

Some of the children's anxiety was directed toward their parents. Could they now be trusted? Might they, too, be capable of doing something so terrible? It's hard to know, some children seemed to be saying. Many children were not willing to take any chances, and suddenly became very "good."

Leslie, age six, conscientiously began to clean her room

shortly after Joshua's death.

According to Molly's mother, Molly had been going through an "Oedipal thing" before Joshua's death. She had told her mother, "I used to love you better, but now I like Daddy better." She took pains to say that she liked, but didn't love, Mommy, and sometimes even hated Mommy. During the period immediately following Joshua's death, however, she kept repeating to her mother that "I think that I really love you better now," and suddenly became extremely affectionate.

Peter became "super well-behaved and cooperative." One Saturday shortly after Joshua's death, he said to his mother, "You know what? I think I should help you with the chores." This was something he had never done before.

Joseph suddenly started giving extravagant compliments to his mother regarding almost everything she did. Her cooking was "delicious," her appearance was "beautiful," and her piano playing was "the best I ever heard, *ever*."

Defying their fears

In an apparent effort to defy their fears, children suddenly began "daring" others to harm them, or playing uncommonly near an open window.

Almost immediately after hearing of Joshua's death, Patrick, age five and a half, began swaying and falling down near the living-room window, crying out, "Look Mommy, I'm falling like Joshua!"

One day shortly after Joshua's death, Sarah, age six and a half, did something naughty. Her mother told her, "You make me angry when you do that." Sarah replied heatedly, "If you're so angry, why don't you just throw me out the window!"

Several weeks after Joshua's death, Steven was being held by his mother in front of a partially open window so that he could see a particularly pretty cloud formation. Suddenly he yelled out half jokingly, "Push me, push me!"

Molly got into an argument with a friend several days after Joshua's death. When various tactics she utilized did not elicit the desired response in her friend, she finally declared that she would simply throw her "out the window."

Sadness

The children's feelings of sadness were expressed in a number of ways.

Patrick frequently and sorrowfully told people that he had lost his best friend, Joshua, and that he now had no best friend. Joshua had died during the Christmas season, and one morning Patrick spoke with his mother about the Christmas tree they would have. He said he wanted to make a special ornament for Joshua, "a red shiny ball," and spoke again of how sad it was that Joshua would have to miss Christmas.

Steven explained to his mother, "When Florence [his pet hamster] died I was half sad—but she was just a pet. When Joshua died I felt *really* sad, because he was a person."

During the days immediately following Joshua's death, Patrick refused to speak to his mother about the various aspects of his life that he used to talk about with Joshua. When his mother asked him about these subjects, he angrily replied, "I could tell my friend Joshua, but she killed him and now I don't have a best friend!"

Steven declared angrily, "Joshua was too young to die. He's not supposed to die that young!"

Molly stated with considerable anger, "I don't believe in God anymore. If he existed, he wouldn't let this happen."

Empathy

Most of the children were able to express or show by their actions their feelings of empathy for Joshua and his father. Virtually every parent in the study encouraged this, almost instinctively realizing that this would help the children cope with their feelings.

Expressing his sympathy for Joshua to his mother, Andrew remarked, "Joshua didn't have a very long life. He was only five, and, you know, you really don't remember the first couple of years very well."

David, age six, confided to his therapist, "When I'm not doing anything I think a lot about Joshua. I wonder how he felt when he fell. Was he scared? Did he feel it? It must have been pretty awful for him."

Molly, upon hearing of Joshua's death, asked her parents, "When is the funeral?" She insisted that she had to go because "Joshua was a child, and he would want a child to be there." She later reflected sympathetically, "He never had his sixth birthday."

Patrick realized that it was hard for Joshua's father to see him soon after the death. He seemed to understand and told his parents, "It's because I was a good friend of Joshua's. I make him remember Joshua, and Joshua is no more."

Donna, age six, said to her mother with concern , "You know, Mommy, I feel bad for that daddy. Now he has no mommy and no little boy."

Several of the children drew pictures for Joshua's dad so he would "feel better."

Parents Respond

Joshua's death caused shock, sadness, and outrage in the close-knit community where he lived. It shook most parents in the neighborhood to their core. Several weeks after Joshua's death, children and parents were predictably still having a difficult time dealing with what had happened. Parents agonized over how an otherwise loving and well-functioning mother could reach the point of killing her child. If it could happen to her, could it not happen to any of them? Children, too, struggled to understand how a mom (who had seemed just like their own mom) could do such a thing. If Joshua wasn't safe, was anybody? At this point, many children experienced predictable symptoms of distress, including sleep problems, loss of appetite, headaches and stomachaches, and regression to earlier behaviors such as bed-wetting.

It would have been both understandable and perhaps expected for these parents to have tried to protect their children from the distressing news by hiding or altering the truth, by trying to distract them from the event, or by asserting that Joshua was happier in heaven than he had been in life. Almost none of the parents I interviewed, however, presented Joshua's death to their children in anything other than an honest way, and all parents took the position that it was, indeed, a horrible, frightening, and unfair thing that had happened. The children received strong and clear messages from their parents that it was perfectly acceptable to be upset, angry, sad, and frightened; that they had every right to feel that way; and that there was no aspect of the death they could not ask about—even over and over again (which many children did).

No parents reported encouraging their children to "be brave." When children cried, many parents, far from discouraging tears, wept along with their sons and daughters. Thus, almost all of the children examined in the study had the opportunity to express and begin to work through their feelings, and they were able to share this process with their parents.

Virtually all of the children studied who knew about the circumstances of Joshua's death seemed to have come through the crisis psychologically intact, with no discernible emotional scarring. My colleagues and I believed that a major reason for this encouraging finding was the actions of the parents, which translate into five basic steps.

Step One: Be honest

Don't lie to children or try to distort the truth in an effort to protect them. Children have an uncanny ability to sense when something is wrong. Lying to them—for whatever reason—puts your children's trust in you in jeopardy should they later find out the truth (which children usually do).

As I discussed earlier, a dilemma for parents in the neighborhood had been whether to tell their children the truth about what had happened. Some parents felt strongly that the need to protect their children from possible psychological trauma outweighed the need to tell them the truth. Others felt that, given the circumstances, it was particularly important to be honest with their children, especially because there was no way of knowing what they might hear from friends and classmates. A month after the death, interviews with parents who had and had not told their children the truth seemed to indicate that the children who knew the actual circumstances of Joshua's death showed more noticeable distress than those who did not. However, after six months had elapsed, the reverse was true: Children who had been told the truth were largely free of the symptoms they had experienced earlier, while children who had not been told the truth were still showing subtle signs of distress. Why was this?

My interpretation, shared by my professional colleagues, was that children who were told the truth had been able to talk and grieve with their parents and ask any questions that they wanted, even if their parents did not always know the answer. The other children, aware that something had happened but not exactly sure what, had no one to talk to about their vague apprehensions. Left to their own devices, their imaginations may well have provided answers that were equally if not more frightening than the truth. There could be no healing or resolution of their fears because those fears had never been dealt with directly.

Step Two: Take your cues from your child

When something violent or frightening happens, start by giving children the basic facts. Do not initially give many specific details. Instead, take your cues from the children.

Wait to see what they want to know. Some children will ask question after question and will want (and need) to know many details. Others will ask virtually nothing. There is not one "correct" reaction. It depends very much on the individual child. Answer children's questions as best you can, with as much sensitivity as possible. If you don't know the answer to a question, tell them that.

Keep in mind that there is such a thing as too much truth. Consider an oft-told tale that sex educators like to relate: A six-year-old boy asks his mother, "Where did I come from?" The mother, wanting to be entirely honest and open with her son, proceeds to give him a detailed explanation of conception, gestation, and birth. After her discourse, the young boy, rather dazed and confused, says to his mother, "But I thought I came from *Cleveland*." The story is a wonderful illustration of how important it is to understand just what your child is asking, and how much she wants and is ready to hear.

Step Three: Encourage communication, but do not pressure children to talk about their feelings

Understand that every child has his own way of coping with frightening events. Some children will need to talk about it continually. For several weeks, Joshua's best friend, Patrick, talked incessantly about Joshua's death. He talked with family, relatives, the postman, the doorman, and the television repair man, among others. Yet other children who were equally upset barely said a word. Sometimes parents are eager and willing to communicate with their children about upsetting events only to find that the children are not at all interested in doing so. "Can

I watch television now?" was a common reply to parents who had hoped to engage their children in a discussion about their feelings regarding the death. In such cases, it's best to respect children's wishes and emphasize that if and when they *do* want to talk, you'll be there to listen.

Step Four: Validate children's feelings

When children are deeply upset, don't try to minimize their feelings or attempt to distract them. It is much more helpful to say, "I can see how upset you are" or "You are right; this is a frightening thing," rather than to assure them that they'll soon feel better or offer them a special treat.

Step Five: Encourage children to think of ways to help those who are hurting

Encouraging children to engage in compassionate acts toward others helps counteract their feelings of helplessness. Reaching out to others also gives children a sense of accomplishment because they have comforted another human being. Joshua's father was certainly very touched by the pictures and cards sent by his son's friends. But the children themselves were also comforted by their own acts of kindness. (See also Chapter One: Fostering Compassion and Courage, for more ideas on helping children to help others.)

Invariably, in the aftermath of a violent event, the most difficult challenge for parents is trying to explain to children *why* bad things happen. How does one answer such questions as "Why does God make people do bad things?" which was recently asked by the five-year-old son of a crime victim?

There are, of course, no definitive answers we can give

to children. But there are ways we can try to address their concerns and confusion. In my children's book, *Why Did It Happen: Helping Children Cope in a Violent World* (Morrow Junior Books, 1994), I tell the story of a young boy, Daniel, who has a special friendship with Mr. James, a neighborhood shopkeeper. One day Mr. James is robbed, and his arm is broken during the robbery. Daniel must struggle with many different emotions and questions about the event. He is helped to cope with feelings of fear, anger, and helplessness by his parents, his teachers, and some of his classmates. But perhaps most of all, he is helped by Mr. James himself, who reminds Daniel that even though bad things sometimes happen, there is much goodness in the world as well, and many ways in which we can be a good friend to people who need our comfort and support.

Several days after the robbery, Mr. James visits Daniel, who has been too afraid to return to Mr. James's store:

> "Are you mad at the man who robbed you?" Daniel asks.
>
> "Yes. I'm mad. But I'm not *just* mad. Because even though that man did a very bad thing, there were other people who were very kind and caring to me. Did you know that a man I'd never met before, who was walking past the store when I was hurt, came inside to see if he could help? Then he drove me to the hospital. And when we got to the hospital, the doctor took very good care of me. She's the one who made this cast to help my arm heal.
>
> "After that my friends came to the hospital to take me home and make me comfortable until my son and daugh-

ter arrived from out of town. And do you know what else?" Daniel shook his head no. "I've gotten notes and phone calls from a lot of people who shop in the store, letting me know that they care. I even got one very special gift." And Mr. James reached into his pocket and took out Daniel's drawing, which he had carefully folded. That made Daniel smile a big smile.

Then Mr. James told him, "It's true that sometimes bad things happen; even to the people we love and care about. And we may never really understand why. It may make us angry or sad or frightened to think about it. But there are things we can do to help people when bad things happen. Just like the help I have gotten. And do you know what else we can do?"

"What?" Daniel asked eagerly.

"We can appreciate the good things that happen—like picnicking in the park, and going sledding in the snow, and just being together with our family and friends who love us. I've especially enjoyed our times together in my store. Would you like to take a walk there now? I can show you all the get-well cards people have sent me, and I sure could use some help filling my jelly bean jars."

"I can help you, Mr. James!" Daniel exclaimed.

"Thank you, Daniel. That means a great deal to me. And so does our friendship."

Later, when he had returned from the store, Daniel thought about what Mr. James had said. He realized that he had helped his friend after all. And it was a very good feeling.

HOW CHILDREN CONNECT VIOLENCE AND DEATH

Young children frequently equate violence with death and destruction. But for many of them the concept of death is, to say the least, confusing. For example, many of the cartoons children watch feature characters who can be pushed off a cliff, run over by a truck, pounded on the head with a hammer, dynamited, and appear to be killed—only to seemingly become alive again, no worse for wear. Early childhood spawns stalwart believers in magic, as children watch and hear stories about ghosts, goblins, and wondrous potions that endow people with magical powers.

During the period our nation was in mourning for the deaths that occurred in the Oklahoma City bombing, a four-year-old asked his mother why the parents of a child who died in the blast were crying. "Can't they wish her back alive again?" he wanted to know.

The New York Times reported that a five-year-old Oklahoma boy, when asked about his reaction to the bombing, replied, "I would tell [Timothy McVeigh], 'You shoot down this building? You put it back together again.' And I would say 'You re-do those people!'"[1]

Consider the answers that a group of six- and seven-year-old youngsters gave to a prominent researcher when he asked the question, "How do you bring dead things back to life?"

> You can't revive them unless you take them to the emergency room and get them doctored up. Then they'll be okay.

Help them, give them hot foods, and keep them healthy so it won't happen again.

No one ever taught me about that, but maybe you could give them some medicine and take them to the hospital to get better.

If you know a lot of science, and give them some pills, you can do it.[2]

Violence in most children's minds is connected with death; someone gets hurt or killed as a result of a violent act. But children's understanding of the concept of death varies widely. In trying to help them cope with the violence they see and hear, it's important to have a sense of just what they think it means to die. This provides an important clue to the kind of anxiety children are likely to experience.

Hundreds of research studies around the world have examined children's perceptions of death. Virtually all agree that whatever their economic or cultural background, children's understanding of death is mainly influenced by their age. In general, children under five years old do not understand that death is final and universal, and that all living things eventually die. So even when a parent or another adult talks about the death of a pet or a relative, it's not unusual for a child of this age to come back to the parent a little while later and ask, "But Grandpa will still come to my birthday party, right?" This doesn't mean the issue wasn't handled sensitively but rather that children cannot fully grasp the implications of death when they are very young, no matter how it is explained.

The Painted Guinea Pig

A well-known story in psychoanalytic literature, "The Painted Guinea Pig,"[3] tells of a nursery-school class whose pet guinea pig, affectionately named Guinny, dies suddenly. Some of the children's parents wanted to immediately replace the pet with another guinea pig who looked exactly the same so the children would be spared the pain of Guinny's death. But the class teacher wisely realized that the death was a "teachable moment" for the children, all of whom must confront death on a regular basis whenever a flower died, someone stomped on a bug, or they watched TV.

So the teacher explained to her students that Guinny had died, and together they mourned Guinny and remembered the many happy, special times they had spent with the pet before his death. Guinny was given a burial in a nearby park, and a period of time passed before the teacher felt the children were ready to accept a new pet. When the time came, she purposely chose a guinea pig that did not resemble Guinny at all; it was a different color and had different markings.

On the day of the guinea pig's arrival, the children ran to get a look at their new pet.

"Look, Guinny's back, Guinny's back!" some of the children called out excitedly, "But someone painted him!"

A less-experienced teacher might have been taken aback

by the children's reaction. Had something gone wrong? Were the discussions about Guinny misleading or not clear enough? Luckily, this nursery-school teacher realized that the children's comments were purely a function of their age. It was hard for them to understand that death was final no matter how it was explained. In the meantime, however, important groundwork had been laid, enabling the children to begin the process of understanding, a process that takes place over a number of years.

In the 1940s, a landmark European study concluded that children from approximately five to nine years of age tend to think of death as a person, a shadowy figure that can be outsmarted or thwarted if children could only figure out how.[4] A number of subsequent studies in the United States, however, have not found this to be so. They report that children of this age, rather than personifying death, tend to have vague and sometimes confusing ideas about the concept. In essence, they "sort of" understand what death means. Most researchers agree that it is not until children are nine or 10 that they are able to fully comprehend the concept of death. It's at this point that children often begin to ponder the possibility of an afterlife, a possibility that often brings comfort. As one nine-year-old told me, explaining her interest in heaven and reincarnation, "You're always *somebody*, you're never *nobody*."

There are exceptions to this basic developmental pattern. Many researchers, clinicians, and parents have observed that certain children as young as two or three seem to fully grasp the meaning of death. For instance, Anna Freud and a colleague reported that a number of British children who had been through the London blitz during World War II and had witnessed the death and devastation caused by the bombings did seem to understand what it means to die.[5] Some very young terminally ill children also have been reported to show an understanding beyond their years. Such children, whether experiencing the consequences of war (including "urban warfare") or illness (as with AIDS, cancer, or other life-threatening diseases), may well have a heightened awareness of death as a biological, universal, and nonreversible process. Most children, however, who are not in imminent jeopardy, tend to need more time to achieve the same level of understanding.

Helping Children Understand Death

In a seminar I recently conducted, a teacher recalled walking into her home when she was six years old and finding everyone in tears. Anxious and fearful, she asked what was wrong. In fact, her Aunt Terressa had just given birth to an infant who had lived for only a few hours. But her mother's explanation to her was that Aunt Terressa had "lost" her baby.

Almost 40 years later, this woman vividly remembered her horror and disappointment that no one seemed to be making an effort to go out and try to find her new cousin. She had nightmares for months, dreaming of this poor, apparently unwanted, lost child. Parents and other caring adults can prevent such confusion and help children develop an understanding of the meaning of death in a number of ways:

- Don't assume that young children understand death as a biological process that is universal and final. If people can die and come back to life in fairy tales and cartoons, why not in real life?
- Never lie to children about death or use euphemisms to explain what has happened. Do not say that the family has "lost" someone, or that the person has gone away or is on a trip, when in reality he or she has died. Covering up causes confusion and mistrustfulness in children, which may persist for years.
- Never compare death with sleeping. Such an analogy may seem to make death appear relatively peaceful and less frightening, but children often confuse these two concepts and may end up developing sleep problems. Is it reasonable to expect children to want to go to sleep if they think this might somehow result in their death?
- Emphasize to children that death is a biological process, and that when people (or pets) die, their bodies stop working and they can no longer move, speak, think, or feel anything. Very young children will not be able to fully grasp this, but explaining it will build a foundation upon which they can begin the process of understanding.
- It's always appropriate to share your religious beliefs with children regarding the existence of a soul or an afterlife. But make the distinction between what is a belief and what is a biological process. While many believe that the soul never dies, the body will not revive itself. Children need to understand this.

Part II
INSPIRATION

Chapter Four
LESSONS ACROSS AMERICA

Many of our country's politicians, social commentators, and poll takers tell us that our country is in moral decline and that we are experiencing a "crisis of values." Yet across America, individuals and communities defy the nay-sayers and poll takers. Perhaps they don't have time to read the polls or listen to the increasingly uncivilized discourse about what constitutes civilized, "moral-based" behavior. They are too busy working to make their communities a better place to live.

They and others like them are hoping to start their own national trend, a person at a time, a block at a time, a community at a time. These special people's actions are communicating to young people that change for the better is possible, and that people of all colors, religions, and economic circumstances should be valued and given a helping hand when they're in trouble.

For example, the actions of thousands of adults in

Billings, Montana, created an indelible impression on the town's children during the holiday season of 1993.

Further west, the lives of dozens of children in San Francisco have improved through the efforts of a single mother and her son. In fact, more than one child would not be alive but for the efforts of this remarkable duo.

On the opposite coast, a small group of children in Boston got a taste of what it was like to work for positive political change, and many more young people started to believe that politics could actually be guided by compassion and morality instead of cynicism—all because of a minister who challenged the conventional political wisdom.

A few hundred miles south, in one of New York City's roughest areas, a nine-year-old boy was inspired by a neighbor's determination to create a place where the community's children could play without fear. Today, 14 years later, that boy presides over a thriving community garden, through which inner-city youngsters are given the chance to make their neighborhood a better place.

Finally, not far away, four adolescent boys in Clifton, New Jersey discovered their capacity for growth and their ability to empathize with others through the efforts of a determined rabbi. His method of working with these young people has inspired the state's justice system to rethink how it handles youthful offenders involved in bias crimes, potentially affecting hundreds, perhaps thousands, of young people.

These true stories are compelling examples of individuals looking within themselves and their communities to find ways of changing a society that many believe needs changing. Their stories, told here primarily in their own words, movingly illustrate how determined people can find ways to make a profound and positive impact upon children.

THE TOWN THAT SAID NO TO HATE: BILLINGS, MONTANA

Acts of hatred and prejudice have always been with us. So, too, have individuals who refuse to accept such acts. Occasionally, a whole community determines to fight against bullies and bigots. This is what happened during the holiday season of 1993 in the town of Billings, Montana.

A stranger walking down Billings's pleasant streets would have no way of knowing that extraordinary things happened there, events that were themselves inspired by people in another place and time.

The basic facts are these:

In early 1993, skinheads and members of racist groups in Billings began distributing hate literature vilifying African-Americans, Hispanics, Jews, and other minorities.

Wayne Inman, chief of the Billings Police Department, and Margaret MacDonald, executive director of the Montana Association of Churches, urged the town's citizens to react strongly and decisively to stop the hate mail. Many people initially thought that the hate mail should be ignored, and that focusing attention on the hatemongers would only serve to encourage them. But Inman and church leaders persisted, starting a series of "teach-ins" throughout the community to educate people about the consequences of not taking a strong stand against hate crimes, even minor ones.

Few people came at first, but attendance slowly grew. Though Inman and the Montana Association of Churches became targets of a series of threats and attacks, they continued to act aggressively.

Educators, human-rights advocates, and labor leaders joined Inman and the churches to form a community network that monitored and forcefully responded to the hate speeches and acts of vandalism against minorities. They published a full-page advertisement in the town newspaper, the *Billings Gazette*, strongly condemning hatred and bigotry. More than 100 community organizations placed their names in the ad, as did thousands of citizens. Community leaders organized a town rally, where the moral equivalent of war against hate crimes was declared.

Things settled down for a while, but more troubling incidents followed. In October of 1993, the house of a racially mixed couple was spray-painted with racial epithets. Within hours, the Billings Coalition for Human Rights arranged for members of the local painter's union to donate their services to repaint the house. The next day, armed with paints and brushes, more than two dozen union members appeared and obliterated the slurs within an hour. They were cheered on and supported by dozens of neighbors and well-wishers.

At about the same time, efforts to intimidate the town's black population intensified. Hate-group members began appearing at the town's African-American Methodist church during Sunday worship services. Taking seats in the back pews, they silently glared at the worshipers. When word of this harassment spread, dozens of members of the

First Congregational Church of Billings and other churches began coming to the Methodist church's Sunday services
to worship along with their neighbors and provide moral
support.

But the acts of hatred continued. As the holidays of
Christmas and Hanukkah approached, the town's Jewish
cemetery was desecrated and the synagogue received a
series of bomb threats. Shortly thereafter, two Jewish
homes displaying menorahs were vandalized. In one of
the homes, the children's bedroom window was shattered
by a cinder block thrown during the night. In both
instances, the children were at home with baby-sitters
while their parents were out for the evening. The
Schnitzer home was one of those targeted. Brian and
Tammie Schnitzer, long active in the local human rights
movement and in their Jewish community, spoke out elo-
quently and forcefully.

Immediately, a network of church and community
groups sprang into action. The Reverend Keith Torney of
the First Congregational Church and Margaret
MacDonald argued forcefully that a meaningful, symbol-
ic gesture from the community was needed in addition to
efforts to apprehend the vandals. MacDonald had an
idea. Inspired by stories she had heard of how Denmark
reacted during the Holocaust, when, as the legend goes,
the Danes were commanded to identify and surrender
their country's Jews, she suggested that Billings's citizens—of all faiths—display pictures of menorahs in their
windows.

Within days, hundreds of families and institutions were
displaying such pictures. At first several windows were bro-

ken in churches and schools. Some cars were vandalized. But these actions only strengthened the town's determination. Soon thousands of menorahs were displayed throughout the town. The *Billings Gazette* printed a full-page color picture of a menorah and urged citizens to display it on a door or window. Thousands more menorahs appeared.

A major business in town replaced its regular advertisement on a prominent billboard with a message strongly condemning the hate crimes. Schools and churches began holding discussions with children of all ages about the events; the talks stressed the dangers of bigotry and the importance of fighting against it. Teachers asked for children's ideas. Many of these children had pictures of menorahs in their own windows and saw their parents taking action against the hatred. Though many had never met a Jewish or African-American child, they started to think and talk about how those children must feel to be the targets of hatred.

When it was time for Hanukkah services to be held in the tiny Billings synagogue, dozens of Christian citizens came to worship with their Jewish neighbors. There was not enough room to accommodate all who came. Many people stood outside the synagogue, ready to protect the worshipers and the synagogue itself.

The fight still goes on in Billings, but the hate speeches, hate literature, and hate crimes have diminished dramatically, at least for now.

In March of 1994, I visited Billings and spoke with the key participants in the events of that past holiday season. I also spoke with many dozens of the town's children. Together they sketched a dramatic portrait of a town coming face-to-face with its conscience.

Dr. Brian Schnitzer and Tammie Schnitzer

For months before the cinder-block-throwing incident, the Schnitzers had been the targets of sporadic threats and intimidation by skinheads and neo-Nazis. The Schnitzers' high visibility as community activists, and their willingness to speak out against acts of hate, resulted in threatening phone calls and hate mail. Perhaps most disturbing, someone had managed to get a list of Brian's patients, several of whom received warnings to "stay away" from the doctor.

> **Brian:** The night the cinder block was thrown through Isaac's window, Tammie and I had been out for the evening, and a baby-sitter was caring for the children. I arrived home first, and the children needed dinner. I started getting them settled and started to prepare the food. I decided, while they were getting settled for bedtime, I would turn down the beds. And I walked into Isaac's room and noticed that the venetian blinds were down about a third of the way or two-thirds of the way. They looked like they had been damaged.
>
> Isaac had done that once before, so I called him into the room and chastised him for playing with the blinds. And he said, "I didn't do it, Dad. I didn't do it." So I let him go, and I turned down the bed and noticed that there was glass all over the place. I pulled up the venetian blinds and saw the hole in the window.
>
> My first reaction was to have somebody take care of the children, protect the children, and to clean the room up so they would not feel threatened. Somehow I thought I could shield Isaac from what happened if I could just

clean up the room. I called our next-door neighbor, Becky Thomas, and she came over and got them dinner and kept them in the living room and in the kitchen. And I cleaned the room. I shook out all their blankets and shook out all the stuffed animals. I vacuumed as much as I could, picked up pieces of the cinder block, put the pieces in a bag, and put the bag out in the garage.

Tammie: By that time he was trying to call me, and he got confused about where I was.

Brian: I didn't know where Tammie was at the time. But, again, my first reaction was to try and protect Isaac. He stepped in and asked what happened. And I said, "Well, it looks like someone threw a rock." And he said, "Bad boys threw a rock?" And I said, "Yes, some bad boys." I didn't want him to think that an adult did it. And then Tammie came home and I told her that I had called the police and reported it, and the police reacted as if it was simply vandalism.

Tammie: I came home and I walked in the door and Brian was in the kitchen and he said, "I need to tell you something." And he took me to the bedroom. It was cold, and he raised up the blinds and there was this gaping hole, and he told me that a cinder block had been thrown through it. I just sat there for a moment, and I said, "Where are the children?" "In our bedroom," he answered. Brian was obviously shaken up, and it was so cold. I'll never forget the coldness.

I became very frightened. I truly just wanted to take my kids and jump in the car and drive away. The only thing that stopped me was that I had nowhere to go. Where would I go? This was ridiculous, and I sat in Isaac's room for the longest time, rocking in his rocking chair. I remember crying, and I remember Brian and I just sitting there. And I said to him that I really needed to understand what happened. Let me just kind of filter this in for a few moments. Then I said, "Brian, did you call the police?" And he said yes, but they considered what had happened to be plain vandalism. I said there are so many people in the police department who don't understand hate crimes, we need to deal with specific people. I said I'll call the police, because I believed we needed to have someone come out to the house.

And so I called the police and asked them to pull up our file. Because, of course, I had taken all the threats we had received to the police. Then they seemed to understand what the problem really was. So they came out, and the policeman said that the first thing we should do is take the menorah out of our window, to protect our children. He said, "Don't leave your children home with the sitter anymore." And he took a bunch of notes and said how the person or persons who did this would have had to be at close range. It was dark outside, but the lights were on inside, so obviously they knew it was a child's room. And it was obvious that they knew that we were gone. They must have been sitting there watching us leave and then they did this.

He asked if our number was unlisted and I said it was, so he said it was obvious that they were following our car, or someone had given them the information. I said, "Yes, you're probably right." We had the children sleep with us in our bedroom that night. We were up the whole time, with our eyes wide open.

Brian: We told the kids to pretend that we were camping out. We had them sleep at the end of the bed in their sleeping bags. But we knew we couldn't continue this indefinitely.

Tammie: After lying there all night long, with my eyes wide open, knowing there was no gun in the room to protect our children and no elaborate security system that was going to protect them from those bricks, I got up the next morning with a great need to tell the world. To just scream out, "Why in hell does my family have to live with this? Do my neighbors have to live with this? Does this neighborhood have to live with this? Why do we have to live with this? This is ridiculous."

I got on the phone at seven that morning. Brian left for work. I called Wayne Sheeley, publisher of the *Billings Gazette*, and got him out of the shower. I said, "Wayne, this has happened to my family and I need help. Please, please, can't we advertise this? Somehow, can you just put it in the paper and let people know about this?" And his response was that I'd be taking a big risk and might be targeted again. And again I said that it didn't matter, that we were targeted already. What did we have to lose at this particular point?

Then I called Jerry Weisman up in Great Falls, knowing that my neighbors were hosting a meeting that Senator Robert Dole was attending, and said, "Please, Jerry, you understand what we are going through here. If you could encourage Senator Dole to come by and take a look at what has been going on, then it would allow me to give him a history of what's been happening. He'll see this not as a broken window; he'll see this as a chain of events, and he'll see this as something that is escalating and will escalate to a point where somebody is going to die. We've got to stop it now."

He immediately agreed. He felt horrible. He asked me to let him help. And we had Senator Dole come by. And then the television stations came by, and I was allowed to show them the window. I talked about how I felt. I said, "If you have a problem with me, you confront me with your issues and I'll be glad to discuss them. But I don't understand, I cannot understand, why you would take it out on my children. I cannot fathom this." It was a plea to the person who was doing this. And that just got the ball rolling, and it kept going on and on.

◆

Tammie: At about this time, one of the neo-Nazi skinheads we'd been having problems with appeared at my door one morning. My son Isaac, who's always vivacious, ran to the front door and opened it and invited this fellow in. Now this fellow had physically threatened my family. It was a shock to see him at the door. He just walked in the house after he was invited in by Isaac, and he stood there.

My daughter was also at home, and I said to him, "What are you doing here?" He said, "I just wanted to see what a Jewish home looks like." And he kind of had a smirk on his face, and I thought to myself, "Okay, Chuck,* this is what a Jewish home looks like. I want you to take a look at this home. Does this home look any different than any other home that you've ever been in?" I

* pseudonym

knew it probably didn't. I said, "Chuck, look at these kids. These are Jewish children, and I want you to tell me you won't do anything to hurt them. Reassure me that you won't harm them." And he just kind of smirked at me again. I said, "Chuck, I know you have a heart and I know you wouldn't let anything happen to them."

Then he walked in and sat down, and I asked the children to go downstairs. Just at that time the phone rang. It was the police chief, Wayne Inman, and I said, "Wayne, I have Chuck Johnson in the house." And he asked, "Are you okay?" And I answered, "I'm fine." I was sitting there thinking, "I don't want to irritate this man." Well, he sat down and I sat down, and I offered him a sparkling water. I wanted to say, "Get out of my house." But that would have given him a reason not to like me or not to understand me. He started looking at some of the Jewish books and he said, "Can you tell me something about Judaism? Do you believe in Satan?" And I said, "No, we don't. I'm not very biblically versed, but I can tell you that I am not raising my children to believe in Satan."

I said, "We eat a little bit differently, and our Sabbath is on Saturday." Then I asked him to give me some background about himself and about his religion. He said he didn't really want to talk about it. He seemed to start feeling a little more comfortable, but I didn't know how stable he was. I said, "Chuck, listen, you've caught me at a bad time. If you could possibly come back at five o'clock, when I'm a little bit more prepared, and I don't have to take my children to school, we can sit and talk." He said, "I have no problem doing that." Then he got up and just kind of reluctantly left.

Shortly after, a bunch of police cars came, and it would have been horrible if they had shown up when he was there. The police advised me not to be home at five o'clock, when he came back. But not to be there at five o'clock? What kind of message would that be sending him? I think that would have been a horrible thing to do. So I made sure my children were not at home, but I was there.

Brian: Tammie and I have a totally different perspective about this. A neighbor called to tell me he was there, and I called Tammie and said I wanted him out of the house; that I would call back in five minutes. I called back in five minutes, and the phone rang and no one answered. You can imagine how I felt. My wife and children were in my house with that bigot. So I immediately called 911 and had them send out the squad cars. That's why they came.

Tammie: I knew how Brian felt, but in my view it was important that I try to meet with this man once more. I didn't know if he had ever actually talked to a Jew before. I thought that maybe talking to him—human being to human being—would make a difference. But when he came back he seemed a lot more violent. He said to me, "If you had half a brain, you'd understand that I am your enemy and you are certainly mine." And I said, "You know, Chuck, I would defend to the death your right to speak what you think. I truly would." Then he said, "You better take me seriously. You understand that I am capable of purchasing weapons. Do you understand that I drive people past your house on a daily basis just to point out your home?" And, of course, I didn't know this. I said, "Chuck, you have to take responsibility for what you are doing. You've been in my home; you've seen me; you know who I am. You know that I am not a problem to you, and that I would never hurt you or stop you from being who you are."

Then he told me that something was going to happen. He wanted me to know that he was not going to be a part of it. And I said, "You are just as guilty if you are inciting this to happen. I feel, now, that the lines of communication are open and I thank you for coming and trying to discuss this with me. But if something happens, there will be no more communication between us."

Then he whipped off his shirt to show me all of these swastikas and tattoos that he had all over his body. And he said, "Take me seriously," and walked away. It was very frightening. I wasn't sure how far he was prepared to go. But it turned out that that visit was essentially his swan song. As it became clear that the community response was becoming stronger and stronger, Chuck literally left town, and he hasn't been heard from since.

◆

Tammie: Of course, Billings responded wonderfully to the cinder-block-throwing incident, but you have to understand that it took years of educating significant people within the community for this to happen. I can tell you that four years ago, the community would not have responded. Brian calls me obnoxious, but I had to become obnoxious in order to be heard.

Brian: The community awareness about hate crimes has now, of course, grown enormously among every segment of the population. After the incidents of vandalism at the synagogue, and the vandalism of the Jewish homes, our rabbi, my son, myself, and a few others went out to breakfast at a local restaurant. The waitress, who was a Native American, asked if we were associated with the synagogue. The rabbi nodded and said, "Yes, we are," and she was very supportive, very nice. When we finished breakfast, she came over and said, "Don't worry about your check. Someone in the restaurant picked it up. We appreciate what you people are trying to do in this town." And the rabbi said, "You know, this has turned out to be an amazing community. Where I come from we might have been harassed on the street. Here they buy you breakfast."

Someone once asked me why this could happen here and didn't happen in Germany in 1936-37. I was trying to figure out why. Because people here are no better than they were there. I'm sure they were no more inherently evil in Germany. And it's certainly not just because of Tammie and me. I think, maybe, there was just the right mix of "combustible materials," and the right mix of people to provide the spark, so to speak. The bottom line is that there are a lot of good people in this town who saw that their neighbors were in trouble. In many parts of the country, certainly back in Virginia, where I come from, people don't know their neighbors. Here they do. That can make all the difference.

Wayne Inman

When Wayne Inman accepted the job of chief of police in Billings, he looked forward to a simpler, less stressful life. Born and raised in the mountains of Montana, Inman had left the state as a young man. Now he envisioned returning to a lifestyle that was closer to nature, with plenty of time to enjoy the outdoors.

Things didn't go exactly as he had planned. Shortly after he came to town, hatemongers began asserting themselves, and Inman became consumed with trying to stop them.

I got a copy of the report explaining what happened to the Schnitzers the following day. I first asked the question, "Is this a crime motivated by hate and a violation of the statute which prohibits vandalism by race, ethnic origin, religion, etc.?" I saw the very same thing happen in Portland, Oregon, and hoped that our community would respond aggressively to these kinds of activities. I had been trying for over a year to get the community out of its denial stage.

I knew the Schnitzers professionally and personally, and I was on the phone immediately. "I'm sorry that this happened," I told them. "It's an act of hate, and I'll go public and call this a hate crime. My organization may not agree with me, and the community may not agree with me. They may call this vandalism, but I choose to call it a hate crime."

I did go public and call it a hate crime. I felt a great deal of anguish for this family. What were they going through?

I was a Portland, Oregon, police department member for more than 27 years. We didn't call them hate crimes there. We had bias crimes, where the targets were the

African-American and homosexual communities. We didn't graduate from hate activity to hate crimes until about the mid-1980s, when we saw the arrival of the skinheads, and they are pretty easy to spot. At first there were a few incidents, then there were quite a few.

They wanted to drive the "mud people"—that is what they call the African-American race—from the community, and they would entertain any method to achieve their objectives. We then saw the harassment of mixed-race couples, gays, and lesbians, and they weren't really very discreet about it. They were very bold. They operated almost with impunity, and the police response at first was to investigate these acts as criminal acts, not as bias crimes. There were quite a few incidents; blacks and gays and mixed-race couples.

The number of incidents over a period of time grew to about 50 or 75 separate instances. We, as a police department, began to tell the mayor and the city council: "We have an emergent problem here. We have seen what has happened in Hayden Lake, Idaho, the headquarters of the Aryan Nation. We have seen what has happened in California. We don't want that to happen here. This is a beautiful city by the river. We have to do something about this before we have a serious injury or death."

I can remember quite vividly being in the mayor's office, and his angry response that this could never happen in his city and that we were exaggerating. It wasn't too long before the community began to pressure for some kind of response to these crimes. But nothing much was done.

Finally, three skinheads were riding in a van. Their avowed intention that evening was to find a "mud person" and kill him. They hunted in the Laurelhurst neighborhood, which is a middle-class neighborhood. An Ethiopian student came out of his apartment, and they saw him and circled the block and confronted him as he was about to get in his car. Then they jumped out with their baseball bats and they harassed and taunted him. They used racial epithets, and one of them punched him and the others kicked him and knocked him to the ground and kicked him with their boots. They then used their bats and they killed him on the spot, for no other reason than that his skin was black. He wasn't even an African-American, as they knew it. He was a man who was from a different country.

We then had a community in shock. How could this happen in the great city of Portland? This is too nice a community for something like this to happen. Why didn't we do something about it before we had a death? That incident was the wake-up call which resulted in a large rally at the site where the man was killed. This involved a couple of thousand people marching to the downtown business district, despite the threats of the skinheads to disrupt the march or even kill somebody. From that time forth, there were a series of activities which sent the message: "We won't tolerate this." From that time on, the influence of the skinheads declined dramatically. It was as if they pushed as hard as they could, and at the point when we finally pushed back they met their resistance. We didn't seem to have any serious incidents after that, although there were some assaults and intimidation.

Until the last couple of years, Montana was not known for its white-supremacy and its hate activity. For the first months I was chief of police here, we didn't have any of this. Then we began to see the presence of skinheads and we began to see their hate literature, and I was thinking, "Oh my God, not again." If there is a term to describe my state of mind then, it would have been outright despondency. I didn't need this and, more importantly, the community didn't need this.

I hoped their presence was nothing more than a presence. But I knew better than that. Every community that had seen the presence of a hate group experiences a progression. We have the presence, we have the literature, harassment and intimidation, moving to vandalism, personal attacks, and then death. I alerted the community, and it was like a voice in the wind. I started to receive my own hate phone calls and letters. They were from the citizens of this community, but they were never signed, and the phone calls were always anonymous.

I received a lot of direct criticism. People said, "You're not in Oregon and these are just a couple of wayward kids who don't deserve the attention that you are giving them. It's a small group, and they can't possibly hurt anything. They haven't committed a crime, so stay out of the social affairs of this community. If you give them attention, they are going to respond to the challenge and do something outrageous. So, police chief, just back off. Get in your office, and leave this alone."

They thought, "We're too nice a community. This is not really happening." Stick your head in the sand, folks. That's exactly what they did. And I said, "I hear you out there. I know you believe that it is not a problem. I know you believe you are doing the right thing. But I must continue to tell you that their presence will result in something terribly devastating to this community, and is it going to take the death of a black man, the death of a Jewish member of the community, or gay or lesbian for you folks to wake up? I will keep talking, keep educating, because once you understand where I am coming from, once you understand that there is a progression to this kind of activity, then you will say, "We won't tolerate this in our community."

I didn't say we were going to drive these people out. I never did use that term. People are guaranteed the right to free speech, but I did say that we have victims in this community who deserve and need our support.

I remember that when the *Gazette* published a story about the skinheads, complete with pictures, there was letter after letter in the Opinion Page saying, "You have done a terrible disservice. These people don't deserve this attention. They are just a small group, and the more you focus on them, the more violent they will become."

Next, I encouraged the community to place a full-page ad in the *Gazette*, decrying hate and bigotry, and to organize a march and a rally. This was May 1993. I had a small group of people who felt, like me, that a strong community response was crucial. Again, our objective was to publicize that we, as a community, were standing up and saying, "We don't accept and will not tolerate hate activities."

The *Gazette* article—actually it was a full-page ad paid with donations—had some 4,000 names and some 100 organizations endorsing a strong resolution against crime, hate, and bigotry. I was able to get a modified resolution through the city council. The big objection, originally, was that the initial resolution talked about gays and lesbians and alternate lifestyles. People were uncomfortable endorsing this, so I lost the scrimmage but won the battle. The council, in full public session, endorsed a modified resolution. Notable entities like the school board of trustees and the county commission and a host of other organizations said in this ad that we don't subscribe to hatred and bigotry.

Then there was a dearth of activity, and there was hardly any literature for weeks. Very few incidents of harassment and intimidation. It was like the manual for the Klan didn't contain a chapter about what to do in the event a community rises up and says, "We won't subscribe to your message of hate and bigotry." This was a first. This community was responding, as a community, to the presence, the literature, the harassment, and the intimidation.

In September, we saw the desecration of the Jewish cemetery, and the officer who took the report left me a copy. Almost incidentally, he left me a copy. I chose to speak out one more time: "This is a crime motivated by hate. This is a crime against the Jewish community." There was criticism again that this was just a bunch of guys who tipped over headstones. It was vandalism. Don't call this a hate crime because you have no evidence. Wrong. A non-Jewish cemetery literally next door was not desecrated.

Hate literature again resurfaced in August and September. I spoke out, and folks still denied it. There was a resurfacing of literature directed toward the Jewish community, as well as blacks, gays, lesbians, Hispanics, and all persons who were not white. Then, in late fall, it seemed like the prime targets became the Jews. There was a lot of rhetoric about the Jewish conspiracy to control the media, to control the international banking system. Billings had yet to get its wake-up call. We hadn't had anything outrageous. We just had a series of incidents, some of which many said were not connected in any way. The wake-up call was the cinder block thrown through the window of the Schnitzers' home.

That incident resulted in an outpouring of support for the Jewish community. I saw menorahs everywhere. I couldn't estimate how many. Thousands were distributed, and most of the outlets ran out and asked how they could get more. I think somewhere near 5,000 were printed, and I would really make the assumption that these 5,000 were posted either in houses, businesses, churches, or in cars. But one thing that is critical to point out is that when the first menorahs were posted, there was retaliation. There were six houses, selected at random, and two churches which were attacked and vandalized, all within one weekend. During the same weekend, there was vandalism at Central Catholic High School. The school had displayed on their billboard, "Let us all get along." They had their window shot out. Some of the victims who had their homes vandalized received phone calls accusing them of being "Jew lovers."

People called and asked, "Is my school safe? Is my business safe? Is my home safe?" And I said I can't guarantee safety, but if we had literally thousands of menorahs out there, we would all reduce our chances of being victims. And besides that, if we allowed this activity to intimidate us to the point where we could no longer speak out because we were afraid of retaliation, then this activity would continue. So we needed to redouble our efforts.

That effort was redoubled, and thousands more menorahs were back in the windows, and there were no more acts of vandalism.

I am truly proud of this community. I saw people respond with loving, supportive responses to hate and bigotry. We have done it right, and I really believe that we have thwarted the efforts of the Klan and the skinheads through active community support. Hopefully, other communities can learn from this.

In 1994, Wayne Inman retired from the Billings police department. He now lives in Oregon and continues to speak out on the importance of aggressively fighting hate crimes.

Margaret E. MacDonald

Margaret MacDonald has been a social activist for much of her adult life. Her social and religious convictions served her well when she became the executive director of the Montana Association of Churches. Courage had not been part of the job description, but that—and some creativity—were what she called upon as the 1993 Christmas and Hanukkah holidays approached.

I was with Tammie Schnitzer the night her home was vandalized. We were having an emergency meeting of the Billings Coalition for Human Rights, and when she got home from the meeting she discovered what happened.

Two mornings later, when I read about it in the newspaper, there was a little something about how the law-enforcement people had counseled the Schnitzers to remove all the Hanukkah decorations from their windows and put up bulletproof glass. Tammie had responded, "You know, that's just a terrible thing to have to do." And that statement just really hit me.

So I was sitting there, trying to think of some way, some really dramatic way, for the community to take action. I was just trying to think what we could do. It was a Saturday morning, and the idea occurred to me that if other people put menorahs in their windows, then the Jewish people would not have to take their menorahs out of their windows, and that would be a wonderful way for the community to help surround the families with support. Because, of course, what had happened affected every Jewish family. They had to be just as terrified even if it wasn't their child. So I called up the pastor of my church, Keith Torney, and said, "Keith, what do you think if we give out menorahs?" Initially, I envisioned doing this with the children, in the children's sermons around the city. I thought there could be discussions with the children about how a family had been the object of hate and bigotry. I also thought that we could tell them the story of what happened in Denmark, about how when the Jews had been singled out for persecution and ordered to wear Jewish stars, the whole community wore Jewish armbands so the Jews couldn't be singled out. Keith immediately said that was a wonderful idea and proceeded to carry it forward.

I'm not sure I would have thought of the idea if

Tammie's statement had not been in the paper. That made me focus on her being asked to take her menorah out of the window, which then made me think about putting menorahs *in* our windows. Had that not been in the paper, I don't think that it would ever have come into my head. It was just kind of an inspiration. Actually, I couldn't remember at first where the story of Christians wearing Jewish armbands during the war had occurred, but I thought it could have been Switzerland or Norway or Finland. Then Keith called me back and said, "By the way, it was the king of Denmark, legend has it, who rode out on his horse, wearing the Star of David, and asked all Danes to do the same." We both agreed the image was very powerful. So then he said "We're going to go for it."

The funny thing is that we were having rehearsals for the Christmas pageant at the church that day. When Keith went in, he saw that the hand-out sheets that had been photocopied for the kids in Sunday school had pictures of menorahs. It was to teach the children about the festival of lights. It was just so perfect.

He spent the day running around, calling churches and running the copies over to them. We both thought that it was almost a cosmic affirmation of the whole idea, that the pictures of the menorahs were already there for us, all copied and ready to hand out.

Eventually, as you know, the pictures of menorahs were distributed all over town. Some schools and churches that put them up were vandalized. But that just made us intensify our efforts. We distributed the pictures of menorahs to the Kwikway convenience stores and some other stores and dry cleaners, to make them accessible to lots of people. And what happened was that we couldn't distribute them fast enough; there was a real demand.

I do remember, however, one objection to our actions. The word had kind of spread out, before the end of the day, and a friend of ours from Congregation Beth Aaron, who comes to our book group at the church and is a good friend, had trepidation about the publicity surrounding this whole business. She contacted Keith and said she would be very concerned about asking children to put the menorahs in their windows because there was a risk involved, a very serious risk. That gave Keith great pause, not to inhibit or censor the idea, but to caution parents and give the menorahs more to the families and to all the people of that church, so that we wouldn't be telling children to put these in their bedroom windows where rocks might be thrown. In fact, as it happened, it was various institutions that had rocks thrown through their windows.

Someone said to me that one of the awesome things about this was that whenever any church or home had been vandalized, checks mysteriously appeared in the mail. People just sent money, anonymously, or wrote checks. This was, of course, totally unsolicited. Keith was very irreverent; he was laughing about how the churches actually made money on the whole business because of all the checks pouring in.

One of the real issues and difficulties we originally had here in dealing with the hate movement was the reluctance and fear on the part of the media about covering the story. Some seemed to feel that this would "feed the beast." We struggled from the start to educate media professionals that if you go out and glamorize skinheads and give them all the press, give them a lot of attention, yes, that does feed the beast. They are right about that. But if you focus on the community's response and report that people are coming to stand in solidarity at vigils, that is the story. That is what the media needs to cover. That's what helps to destroy these groups. It completely undermines the people who are promoting hate because it generally tends to neutralize or demystify their message. It certainly is reassuring and supportive to the people who are being targeted by them.

I know in my heart that what this town did will make a difference to my children, and the other children in the town when they become adults, because I can remember my own parents doing similar things, which at the time I didn't think about too much. I can still remember them talking about McCarthy and groups like the John Birch Society. My folks were saying, "We don't care if everybody calls us Communists, we're going to stand up for civil rights," or whatever it was. I think this has helped me as an adult to deal with these kinds of issues and realize that the world doesn't come to an end if you do what you think is right. My parents risked some ostracism when they stood up for their beliefs. They took some risks. My father, a doctor, may have lost some patients. It didn't really affect our family adversely, but I suppose it could have.

It's not enough to just talk about morals with children. Children have to see you *act* morally. They have to see you do things. You can't just give it lip service. If for no other reason, that was why our community did what it did.

Children must see their parents stand up for other people. I think that is how the world changes. It really does make a difference.

Rev. Keith Torney

The Reverend Keith Torney has never been reluctant to take a stand. Fighting hatred and intolerance is his idea of what being a minister is all about. So when Margaret MacDonald approached him, he immediately promised his support.

There were those who said, "Don't do anything. We always have had this little bunch of haters. Ignore them and they will go away." I think that a lot of churches and organizations wanted to take that kind of stand. In January of 1993, there were some folk who believed that we had to respond to the skinheads and the KKK. Margie MacDonald called us together, and an ad was drawn up for the newspaper that we hoped individuals and groups would sign and sponsor. The ad listed various groups that were being targeted and in effect said that hatred for any group was wrong. In that list, gays and lesbians were mentioned. A lot of people did not sign the ad because gays and lesbians were included.

You see, in the state of Montana homosexuality is a crime. I don't know of anybody who has been prosecuted, but they could be. A lot of so-called religious people have pressured the state legislators not to change this law. Prejudice hits on all levels. After the ad was placed, we participated in a community-wide "March Against Hate." About 500 or 600 people participated. It was a mix of the whole community—church groups, interested individuals, labor groups, a gay community group—all kinds of people. The Klan called us a bunch of misplaced hippies, but we were really people supporting justice for all.

After the desecration of the cemetery, the bomb threats against the synagogue, and the rocks through the windows of Jews, more and more people understood that we could not be quiet on this issue. It was suggested by somebody that the Jews take their religious symbols out of their windows. That suggestion made me even more angry and more determined than before. Margie MacDonald called to talk about ways that we could show support.

I think what happened with this whole menorah thing is that permission was given for people to be good. People are often told that, but in this case we gave them a way to do it. All kinds of people put up menorahs, like the little old ladies over on D Street with plate-glass windows and no family. Wow! What a risk they took. In a sense, they were helpless. When the Schnitzers' home got hit, we all knew they were very capable people. I'm not sure about these other people. These other people were really afraid. They weren't mounting a huge human-rights campaign; they just felt that this was the right thing to do. To me, that's very impressive.

If I have wept over this at all, this is where I have been most touched, by the people that I know whom I've seen participating. They had the courage to say, "I'm a Jew." Because that's what they were saying. Each one had to do it. It wasn't that someone was going to come and put their glass window back in if someone vandalized it. There was no guarantee.

People would tell me, "I'm afraid. I've got little kids." I would have to say, "I understand that. I don't put you down for that." I think the amazing thing about this town was that people struggled with it. Never again will people just accept bigotry and think, "Yeah, that's the way the world works; you just shove people around." Even people who may have been peddling some of that hate might have gotten the message that the world doesn't automatically accept that hatred is the way of the world. That's exciting. Kids need that model. Kids need to know that goodness is better.

It's almost embarrassing about this story. It's not the Garden of Eden here. We have huge problems. But people are trying. I think this could happen in any community. I used to live in Chicago, and I have so many stories of people reaching out there in ways that you wouldn't expect. This town is a little smaller, the air is a little cleaner, but I think this is every place. It's not unique here. If it is, we are all in big trouble.

There's an Indian word, *Ondinok*, that means "the benevolent desires of the soul." The Iroquois believe that if those desires aren't allowed to come out, you get sick. I believe a lot of sickness is caused by the inability to express goodness. What we did in Billings was give people the ability to express goodness. And they responded in a way no one could have anticipated.

Readers may want to note that my book, *The Christmas Menorahs: How a Town Fought Hate* (Albert Whitman, 1995), recounts the story of Billings especially for children.

SPREADING THE POLITICS OF HOPE:
BOSTON, MASSACHUSETTS

Reverend Robert Massie, Jr., had had enough. The Episcopal minister and Harvard Divinity School teacher decided that it was time to challenge conventional politics. During the heated 1994 elections, when most politicians were shrilly decrying what was wrong with America and focusing on the issues that divide us, Rev. Massie began his campaign of the heart. As a candidate for the office of lieutenant governor of Massachusetts, he spoke of the need for compassion, courage, and renewal. He spoke, as well, of his personal journey through pain to experience joy, hope, and a deep connectedness to others.

Starting as a total unknown, without a political organization to back him, Rev. Massie was able to touch the hearts and minds of an often skeptical, weary, and frightened electorate. His vision of a better society has transformed and activated young and old across the state.

As a child, Rev. Massie suffered from severe hemophilia, which caused him excruciating pain and required hundreds of blood transfusions. (Now, in his late thirties, his condition has stabilized.) Growing up, he had to cope not only with hemophilia but with the stigma of being "different." Fortunately, he had the help of two remarkable parents and his own inner resources and faith. Eventually the transforming experience of his childhood led him to the ministry and, recently, into the rough-and-tumble world of politics.

Being different. What does that mean? So many children, so many adults struggle today with a sense of being set apart, of not meeting society's expectations and falling short of its ideals. In Rev. Massie's case, he and his family had to contend with the consequences of a chronic, debilitating condition in a culture that worships health and physical perfection. He recalled the experience in a recent interview.

Rev. Robert Massie, Jr.

I had a very unusual childhood. On the one hand, it was marvelously privileged. I was a white North American with educated parents who, although not wealthy, knew how to survive in a competitive world and were devoted to solving the problems we faced because of my hemophilia. They did extraordinary things and attracted an extraordinary network of friends. So my childhood was a very exciting and interesting time for me.

On the other hand, it was also a time filled with loneliness and pain, difficulty and frustration. I grew up with a sense of living in two worlds: of being both privileged and rejected. I was a kid with braces who couldn't participate in many things and who was often rejected because of my appearance; because I was different. In my heart of hearts, I came to identify with people who are also marginalized, whether it was because of race, poverty, or any one of a number of handicaps. This has certainly motivated a lot of my actions.

But other things motivated me as well: my parents, my faith, and my belief in God. I believe that it is possible for each of us, whatever our personal dragons, to come through our pain to experience joy. To do that, we have to learn to connect with one another. The problem is that each person is born in a different place, part of a different family, with a different personality. We have a totally different set of experiences, strengths, and weaknesses. We face a different set of difficulties. It's so easy to feel that we are unique in our experience, particularly if we are suffering.

We're living in a world where we tend to focus inward, on ourselves or our own particular group. We come to feel that only people from our own group will be able to understand us or empathize with us. We then tend to form subgroups within those groups. If this trend continues to its logical conclusion, we will each end up as a subgroup of one—standing in radical isolation from one another.

I've come to a point where I strongly believe that instead of insisting our own suffering is unique and incomprehensible to everyone else, we can actually use our suffering to connect with others. I realized that I could make a leap from my experience of physical pain, loneliness, and rejection to how others felt; that there was a kind of basic connectedness through the experience of suffering itself. It was a very powerful insight for me, because I suddenly realized that I felt a deep understanding and love for many, many other people who were experiencing pain. I knew something of what they were going through, despite their particular circumstances.

Within the biblical tradition there is a rich set of resources for seeing the world that way, and for trying to build upon a communal experience and reach out to others. That was an important concept for me as I began the process of becoming a minister.

Eventually I was ordained in the Episcopal Church, and I served in New York City for several years. I got myself in trouble there, because I couldn't understand how one could have a beautiful building, a $9 million endowment, and a congregation that was purporting to be followers of Christ, while ignoring homeless people who were sleeping on the church steps every day. I was the chaplain of the church school and had a wonderful time teaching the children. But I kept thinking that a church has to be more than a place where people come on Sunday or on holidays to talk about their spiritual values. So I prodded the church hierarchy, and we ended up opening up a shelter, which we expected to be temporary. Sadly, it's still in existence because the need continues. We also became involved with one of the first Habitat for Humanity sites in the New York City area. We just did our best.

My actions were motivated in part because of my awareness that the children in the congregation were troubled by what they were seeing around them—the homelessness and poverty. For the most part, these were children from privileged families. There was a dramatic contrast between their lives and what they were seeing on the streets. This was about 1982, and homelessness was really beginning to surge. Youngsters were troubled that so many adults seemed to be ignoring it. You know, adults telling them, "Don't worry, dear, this isn't a problem," while they stepped over people on their way to school. The children needed to know that the adults around them cared.

When I was a child, I would look through different

books that my mother and father brought home. One of them was a book about India. I was fascinated by India. I've still never been there, but I would love to go some day. Anyway, in the book there were some incredible photographs of exotic places. One particular photo grabbed my attention, a photo of the streets of Calcutta. There were people on their way to work, and there were all of these other people lying on the street. Everyone seemed to be just walking by, not noticing. I remember thinking how could one ever live in a society where you walk past human beings who are suffering all around you? I just couldn't imagine how that could take place. I thought, this would never happen in America. We could never do that. And so when I began to see it happening as a young minister, it was deeply, deeply troubling.

The problem with looking at large issues of justice and morality in a society, generally, is that people become overwhelmed. They become so aware, on some level, of their guilt and complicity that they say, "I can't handle this," and something inside them shuts off. But within most religious traditions, certainly within Christianity, there is a mechanism of forgiveness, so that we recognize that yes, we *are* under judgment for not doing all of these things that we know we should be doing, but at the same time we are also forgiven and free to go back and try again. That's what we have to communicate to children; that we all must try, whatever our flaws or failures.

One day in 1984, during a routine medical exam, I discovered that I was HIV-positive. Like many other hemophiliacs, I had contracted it from the blood factors I had been using to transfuse myself. I was already aware of the finiteness of life. The knowledge about HIV just heightened that sense: that there were going to be a certain number of breakfasts left, a certain number of lunches and dinners, a certain number of times I would tie my shoes, laugh at a joke, or watch the snow fall.

Strangely, rather than having a sense that I was being deprived, I found that the limited time I would have left to experience those actions sanctified them all the more. I don't want to gloss over the complexity of the experience, or the pain, but I did definitely find myself appreciating things with an unusual intensity.

There are a lot of things in life that are beyond our control. If we let that overpower our sense of wonderment, then we are in trouble. I find I have been more bold, in the sense that I have done things where the risk of failure is much greater, than I would have been able to tolerate before. I went and got a doctorate at the Harvard Business School, with no business training at all. I survived it, and I did well. But I didn't know I would succeed when I started. In the past, if I had felt that doing something like that might lead me to fail and possibly be humiliated, I probably wouldn't have taken it on.

I ended up writing a long and passionate book about the United States' relations with South Africa. It was insane to think that I could ever write such a big thing, but I did. And, you know, I've been polishing it up and it's going to be published this year. It was an act of love and of conviction.

I also don't think I would have run for office before I received the HIV diagnosis. But I really felt that I could no longer stand the way politics was going in America. I had just come back from South Africa, where people had been through terrible, terrible times: economic injustice, racial hatred, torture, and murder. But people there were coming together under the belief that through dialogue, conversation, and the peaceful ballot box, they could define common goals and common principles and build an entirely new society. It was absolutely thrilling to see. And it was based on nothing more than their conviction that they could do it. They believed in this so much that it was, in fact, actually happening. Then I came back to the United States and saw an angry and frustrated electorate and a crew of cynical politicians. I thought, this is disgusting. How could we have gotten to this point in Massachusetts, the birthplace of democracy in America? I thought it was an outrage, and I felt a tremendous inner urge to step out and do something.

The funny thing was, I really didn't know whether that inner urge was a temptation or a calling. I had to go through a long evaluation and discernment process to know for sure. I talked to a lot of people and looked at all the angles that I could think of. Finally, it just came down to a strong inner sense that even though I didn't know how far I was going to get, it was worth doing. HIV certainly played a role in my decision. I couldn't delude myself by saying, "Well, I'll wait eight years or 12 years. Maybe I'll be more ready to do this then." I had a strong feeling that life had to be lived *now*.

The agenda of a lot of politicians during the last election was to make people more frightened about the future. When we are afraid and anxious, that enables us to harm each other in all kinds of ways. This is what I found so demoralizing. I was determined to fight against this. The debate, as framed by the Republican incumbents, was about crime, welfare, and taxes. Those are the things that people are afraid of or angry about, and that's all the politicians ever talked about. You know: "We will get back at those terrible welfare people, and we will protect you from all those thousands of evil criminals who are going to get you. We will stop people from stealing your money."

I tried to be more positive. I admitted that we've done some things wrong. But I told people that the biggest thing we've done wrong is to make people believe that we can't make our society a better place. The politicians were basically managing decline rather than building something new.

It was amazing how enthusiastically people responded to my message. There were a lot of young people in my campaign. The youngest was seven years old. We had to get 10,000 signatures as part of the process of getting on the ballot. That little first grader would be out there, at shopping centers, running up to people and telling them why they should support my candidacy. He understood what I was trying to say. I think I was tapping into a basic human need that people of all ages experience.

I believe that one of the most important lessons that parents can pass on to their children is that the future can be better than the past. People used to believe in progress. They felt that without any human effort, through the natural forces of history, things were just going to get better on their own accord. And now, when you listen to people, you hear a lot of opinions that through the natural forces of history, things are simply going to get worse. What we have lost is what has historically made the United States so special: the conviction that average people can determine their own future through a process of conversation, discussion, and making decisions through the voting process. We have lost that belief.

One of the things that is most disheartening about politics today is that politicians have generally chosen to emphasize how bad things are getting and how it really ultimately comes down to protecting ourselves from these terrible forces. They try to persuade people that it's all hopeless and try to instill a sense of futility. It's not just politicians who do this. Leaders of many other big institutions encourage the notion that people don't really matter, except as consumers, perhaps, but not as citizens. We must constantly remind ourselves *and* our children that what we become depends on what we believe. If we *believe* that things are going to get worse, often they do get worse. If we believe we can make a difference, then that belief begins to come true, too. The amazing thing is that it really doesn't take very many people to believe in change for changes to begin to be made.

Instead of focusing on the negative, think what our country would be like if families sat down and talked together about how our immediate communities could be better, and what we each could do to help make that happen. If every family committed to doing that on a regular basis, you would begin to see things happen. If every parent asked their children, "What do *you* think we should be doing as a family to make our neighborhood better?" they would get ideas back. The more people actually talk about what kind of community they want to live in, and the more they can visualize it and see what it might be like, the more likely it is to come true.

On the other hand, parents' negative messages to their children have just as much impact. I'll give you an example. During the signature period of the campaign, when I was trying to get enough names to get on the ballot, I traveled from signature site to signature site just to say hello to people and to encourage the volunteers. At one point, we stopped at an upscale health-food store. I was greeting people as they came out, and I was struck that most people were a little cool towards me compared to some of the working-class neighborhoods I had been in. I approached a man who was standing on the sidewalk with his groceries, waiting for someone to come pick him up. He was standing there with his three sons, whom I remember as being about three, five, and seven years old. They were all rather close in age, and small. He himself was a very handsome, well-groomed man. There was a sense of affluence and success about him. When I approached, I said, "Hello, my name is Bob Massie." He turned to me and angrily shouted that I should get away from him. I was startled and said that I just wanted to say hello. He answered furiously, "I don't want to talk to you." Frankly, when I'm in situations like that I can get pretty stubborn, so I persisted and said, "Why not?" And he sputtered, "Because you're a politician." He almost spat the words out. And then he said, "All politicians are liars," and some other things to that effect. His anger and contempt were palpable. As this was happening, I noticed that his children were closely watching us. What were they learning? I wondered. I thought about that incident for weeks and became even more determined to involve kids in my campaign in whatever way I could so they could experience the political process and not grow up to be contemptuous of it.

Actually, from the very beginning of the campaign, I had rejected the notion that only political professionals had something to offer, or that they should automatically be in control of the campaign. To me, that perspective was precisely what gets so many campaigns in trouble. I believed that the more I had teenagers and children and seniors and others around to give the campaign a sense of a group effort, the more the campaign would grow in strength.

That belief probably came from my background as a minister. The congregation of my church in Massachusetts never had much money. What they could mostly contribute to our church projects was their time and their ideas. In order to encourage them to do that, I tried hard to make the church a very family-friendly place. Young people were always around and welcomed. And that eventually translated into how I campaigned.

Ultimately I lost the general election. But my victory in the statewide primary astonished the political establishment. We had started out with no money, no organization. I was a complete unknown. But people responded to a message of hope, of less division and more connectedness, and of a vision of what is possible.

A big part of the reason I ran this race was for young people—my own and everyone else's. They're growing up with an unrelenting barrage of messages of hatred, violence, and pessimism about the future. We can give them so much more.

My young sons were very proud of me for running. They were just seven and a half and five and a half during the campaign. But they sensed what it was all about. They knew that I was fighting for something important, and they saw their father do something bold—despite a lot of trepidation and anxiety—because he thought it was the right thing to do.

I have to believe that no matter what happens, my sons will remember that.

A Different Childhood

In their deeply moving book, *Journey* (Knopf, 1973), Rev. Robert Massie's parents, Robert and Suzanne Massie, wrote about the experience of raising a child with a serious chronic condition while living in a society that so values physical perfection.

Robert Massie wrote:

> The creation of a child is a miracle. I remember once hearing a doctor say that he never lost his sense of wonder at what happens in the delivery room. "There are four people in the room and then, suddenly, there is a fifth person, a brand-new, freshly minted human being."
>
> New, pure, perfect, filled with infinite potential, a newborn child is a miracle of God. I believe this. Who created it, if not God? Where did it come from, if not from God? . . .
>
> If a healthy child is a perfect miracle of God, who created the imperfect child? Why would God create imper-

fection? Especially in a child? Especially in our child?

The doctor had said, "The child has classical hemophilia." And yet, there in his crib next to our bed, cooing happily, lay this beautiful little boy. A classical hemophiliac. My son. Bobby. Two thoughts raced in circles through my brain. It can't be true. It is. It can't be. It is.[1]

Suzanne Massie remembered:

At home [Bob and I] had already made the decision that Bobby was going to be treated normally. The long-range medical prognosis was that Bobby, depending on luck and circumstances, could have a normal life span. That could apply to any of us. The disease was most dangerous and destructive in childhood, but, we were told, after eighteen, when a boy has passed puberty and completed his physical growth, it seemed to be less active. Not that he would escape all problems thereafter, but they were likely to be less frequent. To reach that physical goal of adulthood in the best possible health was one of our two objectives for Bobby. The other, just as important and maybe even more important, was that he reach adulthood in good psychological health. Bobby was a curious, inquiring, outgoing boy with a happy nature. It was our job to protect these God-given qualities and never permit them to be crushed. It was we who had to help him fulfill the promise of his luminous personality, and bring him to that distant plateau as a vigorous, outgoing adult. If, at the end of the struggle, he was to emerge and live in a normal world, Bobby had to be taught to accept and understand prejudice, then to fight it, and finally to be strong enough to ignore it.[2]

The Massies found that the battle to protect and nurture Bobby's physical and psychological health was heightened by our culture's attitude toward illness and disability. Suzanne Massie explained:

> We had thought of ourselves as being just the same, except that this problem had happened to us. But we began to see that the rest of the world did not share our view. In their eyes, we were no longer like everyone else. Somehow we had changed. An invisible barrier had been erected and we were on the other side. We were no longer normal.
>
> Why is it that we in America are so afraid of disease?
>
> People were always afraid of us. I could sense this. It was as though they felt that we had been touched with a curse and that too close contact might contaminate them or give them a glimpse of an unpleasant reality they wanted to avoid having to face . . . .
>
> Early in our experience I realized that the world would accept us—and—Bobby only to the extent that we did not bother them too much . . . . We had to remake ourselves in their image; they did not reach out to understand our world. Our world frightened them, with its echoes of pain, helplessness, and desperation.[3]

More than 20 years after the publication of *Journey* (which is still in print, in a Ballantine paperback edition), Suzanne Massie reflected on what had sustained her, and how she tried to help sustain her son, during the crisis-laden years of Bobby's childhood and adolescence.

Suzanne Massie

Both my parents were Swiss. My father, particularly, was quite a stern man in his way, but he had some very, very strong principles. Among them was that an individual decides how he or she is going to live. Nobody makes you. You make you. He always said that every individual in the world can make a difference. He developed in us a very, very strong sense of being self-reliant. When my sisters and I were little and we'd ask him "How do I do this?" or "What do I do now?" he'd usually answer, "Figure it out for yourself." And so we usually did, in fact, figure it out for ourselves.

From the time I was six years old, our family spent at least part of each summer on the rustic, beautiful island of Deer Isle, off the coast of Maine. We had a small cabin with no running water and an outhouse. We used kerosene lamps and pumped all our water from a well. We didn't have any modern conveniences.

In Deer Isle, nature was clearly the dominant force. Most of our neighbors were lobster men and their families. The sea was their livelihood. They didn't live by the clock, they lived by the tides. And they understood, so well, that nature can be capricious. It can sometimes be cruel. Sometimes there were accidents. No one expected perfection from nature.

That's why I felt so strongly that no matter what medical problems Bobby might be experiencing, during any given summer, it was crucial for him to experience life at Deer Isle, where he was not the medical "oddity" he tended to be back home. For illness, accidents, and aberrations have always been regarded as the way of the world on our island. It's seen as part of the scheme of nature that cannot always be understood. People took Bobby's illness in their stride.

During each of his summers at Deer Isle, Bobby was surrounded by butterflies and insects and grasshoppers and frogs. He was able to see the way nature worked. And feel a certain sense of mastery in being able to be resourceful in this kind of environment. He carried that sense of pride and self-confidence back with him when we returned to New York. And it was truly a gift.

Apart from nature, I would say that my religious faith had a very profound impact on myself and Bobby when he was growing up. My parents were not particularly religious, but they were Swiss and they were Calvinists. They wanted their children to have a decent moral upbringing, so they sent us to the local Presbyterian church. It's the closest you can get to Calvin. So we went. However, as soon as I grew up and studied history, I was absolutely outraged by the way John Knox had treated Mary Queen of Scots. I thought that was just terrible. So by the age of 21, I had become an Episcopalian.

I made a pretty good stab at going to church, but when we began our battle with hemophilia my faith was severely tested. I wanted to go to church, but I couldn't find anything there to help me spiritually. I'd sit there and be glad to just have an hour of peace, but I couldn't connect in any way. There was nothing happening, really, except that I was having this time of peace.

I had been attending services regularly, and after a while I mustered up the courage to approach the minister and ask him if I could please ask the congregation if anybody who was routinely giving blood might give blood for Bobby. At that time, Bobby needed blood desperately for the transfusions that were keeping him alive. However generous our families and friends were, in this regard they couldn't possibly fill the need. We were constantly preoccupied with collecting blood, so I shyly asked the minister if perhaps he might let me put up a small notice about Bobby.

"Oh no," he told me. That was out of the question. If he said yes to me, who knew how many other people might want to make appeals?

Well, I walked out of that church and didn't go back. But I felt a great lack; a longing to be connected to something outside myself and my family. I have a friend, an artist I met in Russia, and he says that nobody ever died crying out for atheism. And this is true, I think. Our religious faith fills a very crucial need, particularly when we have a situation which is beyond our control. When we cannot do anything, it's very scary. Finally, we have to trust that there is some reason for what happens to us and that we are not alone. But it took me quite a while to reach that point. I was very bitter. I had sort of barricaded myself off in my own world.

Then one day, at a cocktail party, after our family had moved to another town, a local minister approached me. He had heard about Bobby and wanted to know how he could help us. "Come see me," he said, "and we'll talk."

I was polite but had no intention of following up on his offer. Fat chance, I thought, of letting myself be hurt and rejected by the church again.

Some time passed, and then I ran into the minister

again. "Forgive me," he said. "For what?" I asked, a bit startled. "For my asking you to come to me. It was I who should have come to you."

The very next day, without being asked, he and some of his congregants began to organize a blood drive for Bobby. That sent me back to church. And this time it was different. You know, so many of us, if we go to church or synagogue and don't feel anything, are convinced that it's because there's nothing there. But the fact is, if people would put as much time into developing their spiritual life as they put into developing their muscles at the health club, they'd get something. I mean, you don't get something without putting something in. You don't become a ballet dancer unless you do a barre every day. You have to do exercises. You can't expect that your legs are suddenly going to turn into a beautiful ballet dancer's legs unless you work at it. And you're not going to have a spiritual life unless you work at it. Finally, I decided to work at it. And my faith has helped sustain me ever since.

Ironically, during the time that I felt personally estranged from the church, I continued to send Bobby to Sunday school. I did it, frankly, so that Bobby could have some companionship. He was becoming more and more socially isolated because of the long periods he couldn't attend school, and because people were so afraid or so ignorant of hemophilia. No recreational programs would take Bobby, the Boy Scouts had rejected him, so finally I thought, "Well, I'll take him to church. They have to accept him there." They did, and ultimately, of course, he became a minister.

Bobby's faith sustained him many times during his

growing-up years. It helped make him the kind of person he is today and gave him a sense that there was a place for him in the universe and that there was a powerful, loving force that cared about him and others. Given what's going on in the world, I believe that children today especially need this kind of faith.

There is one other element that was very important in Bobby's emotional and moral development. Bob's father and I had a basic rule: no self-pity. That isn't to say that Bobby couldn't talk to us about his feelings—and certainly there were times he felt despair or anger or great frustration. But we didn't encourage this business of "Woe is me, I'm worse off than anybody else in this whole world."

Actually, it's very hard when you have a child with hemophilia, or any chronic condition, not to allow him or her to feel sorry for themselves or make excuses. Of course, you see their suffering and you want to spare them. But basically you can't do that. I remember summers in Maine when Bobby was confined to a wheelchair and couldn't walk. When he went clamming with the other kids, he'd have to literally crawl around on his bottom. We could have said, "Oh poor Bobby, he can't walk, and he has to go clamming crawling around on his bottom." But, you know, there he was clamming with the others, and *he got clams*. It didn't matter how he got them, and that's what we focused on.

Bobby might not be able to play football or baseball, but I taught him to cook, which kept his fingers and his head occupied. And Bobby taught himself to play the guitar, which provided company and also drew people to him when he was in a crowd. It helped, in some ways, to combat the loneliness.

One of the things I feel most strongly about is that if we have terrible problems, and we're feeling very sad, the best way to get over it is to go out and try to help somebody else. That's what I tried to stress to my children, including Bobby. But it's really important how we go about trying to help people. I had learned so much from our own situation, you see. Nobody wants pity, but we all need human compassion and understanding.

During the worst times of our battle with hemophilia, when Bobby was often in excruciating pain and there was very little money or time for anything but dealing with this condition, people would come up to me and say, "Poor Sue, I don't know how you do it." Well, this immediately puts a wall between you and that person. Compassion means saying, "I know it must be very hard for you, and that you must be going through some difficult things. Can I help?" And then, "*How* can I help?" That has to be the next question.

There were some mothers who would say to me, "You know, I'd love to have Bobby come over and play with my son. But I just don't know what I'd do if my little Johnny hit him on the head." Well, frankly, that's not the problem with hemophilia, unless some really crazy kid who's out of control comes along with a baseball bat. But they didn't want to know that. What they were saying was, "I don't want the responsibility. I don't want to become involved." They could have said instead, "Tell me what I need to know before Bobby comes over to our house." Some people did say that. And it was wonderful when that happened. It made a world of difference—both to me and to Bobby.

The Littlest Campaigner

As Massachusetts residents went about their business during the 1994 election season, many of them found themselves approached by an earnest volunteer from the Massie campaign. "Please, can you sign this petition for Bob Massie?" they were implored. "We *need* him."

The volunteer then spoke knowledgeably about the candidate's position on a number of issues, especially health care. Some people were rather surprised by this particular campaign worker, who was four feet tall and possessed of a winsome, gap-toothed grin.

Seven-year-old David Yust-Schutt had a mission that fall. He was determined to help elect the candidate for lieutenant governor who genuinely cared about people. And that candidate, he was convinced, was Bob Massie.

"As parents, we often talked with David about our belief that we're all responsible for working toward the goal of a better, more just society," says David's mother, Reverend Karen Yust, an ordained minister who teaches with Rev. Robert Massie at the Harvard Divinity School. "We spoke of my husband's and my conviction that each one of us can make a difference—or at least that it's important to try. And we discussed some of the principles that Bob Massie stands for, explaining to David that these are our principles, too."

David's father, Brady Schutt, adds: "We've always tried to communicate to our son the importance of thinking about what's best for everybody, not just our own family. We told him why we thought it was important to work on the campaign, and he was very eager to help."

When David is asked to talk about the reasons he wanted to become involved, he answers: "Well, I don't like all the violence everywhere. And I think that people should be able to go to the doctor when they're sick, even if they don't have a lot of money. Someone might have a bad accident or something. You never know."

And just how did David think Rev. Massie could begin to solve these problems? "He could help make new laws," this seven-year-old veteran campaigner points out.

"Bob ran a very child-friendly campaign," Rev. Yust recalls. "Children and their families were encouraged to become part of the effort. David stuffed envelopes, held up signs, and was dauntless in trying to get signatures for our petitions. He was very effective. Adults hated to turn him down. Some people actually apologized to him for not signing, and explained that they couldn't because they weren't registered Democrats."

"He amassed almost as many signatures as I did," Mr. Schutt adds. "Sometimes adults will listen to kids in a way that they won't listen to other adults."

When Rev. Massie lost the election, David was disappointed, but he knew that he had accomplished something special. His enthusiasm for politics is undiminished. "He keeps asking Bob when he's going to run again," says Rev. Yust. "He knows that we can't give up the fight. But just as important, he knows that his help was valued. Bob, and others in the campaign, always treated him with respect. His ideas were listened to, and no one talked down to him. Kids need to be treated that way—and not just during political campaigns."

David says there are a couple of things that he especially liked about being a part of the campaign. "Meeting lots of different people was the very best thing," he remembers. "But the Peter, Paul and Mary concert [held as a fund-raiser] was pretty good, too!"

SHOWING CHILDREN SOMEONE CARES: SAN FRANCISCO, CALIFORNIA

For more than a decade, mother and son Ruth and Brian Jackson have worked to bring a better life to the children of their rough San Francisco neighborhood. Although the problems of their neighborhood—like those of every inner-city community—may seem insurmountable even with outside help, Ruth and Brian have labored from within, offering the children perhaps the one thing they need most: role models. Brian and Ruth, whose efforts are becoming known throughout the San Francisco area, form a virtual community center/social service agency/grassroots political organization. Although they live in a community that has more than its share of problems, the Jacksons have dug in their heels and remain committed to saving their neighborhood—especially its children. They discussed their work in a recent interview.

> **Ruth:** We live in a community called Visitacion Valley. It's a very rough neighborhood, what you'd call the inner city. Our house stands between two giant housing projects. Down the street is a corner that's supposedly the worst corner in San Francisco, because that's where all the drug

dealers and crack kids hang out. I think it was about '78 when I was passing the corner and saw a young child, about seven or eight years old, making a drug transaction.

That really shook me up. I thought about how it could have been my child making that deal—anyone's child. I knew I had to do something, so I wrote to the mayor. But she didn't respond. The truth is, politicians have been ignoring this neighborhood for years. It's predominantly black, and the people are poor, and there are a lot of problems here. A lot of people just kind of wish we'd all go away.

Finally, I began to realize that we couldn't depend on the politicians. All we could depend on was ourselves. And that we'd better start trying to do something on our own, fast. Because we were losing these kids to guns and to drugs. And pretty soon there would be hardly any kids left. I really believed that. So I began to speak to some of my neighbors, mostly women with kids. There was one particular woman named Levaugh King. She and I started to organize some community meetings, and we joined an organization called the African-American Community Agenda. And we began to rally. You know, trying to get people involved.

At that time, the organization had just been started. It was very grassroots, made up of people who were determined to try to save the black young men who were dying in the streets. Basically, we did anything we could think of to rouse the community and get the city officials to recognize that our kids were dying. We did a lot of talking and a lot of yelling. We started demonstrating—maybe not in very big numbers, but enough to be a nuisance and to at least get ourselves heard. We formed a group called the

Visitacion Valley Parents for Youths. And the group made a commitment to support my son Brian's work with our neighborhood kids.

Brian: Well, I was about 20 years old and in college part-time when I first started getting involved with the kids in the neighborhood. I had been looking back at my past, especially my early years, and I realized that I had spent a lot of time looking for a male role model to connect with, somebody to basically show me the way. My father wasn't around, and there were no men that I could really talk to or who would play different sports with me.

I began noticing that when I was in the streets playing basketball or other sports or just hanging out, kids started gravitating toward me. They asked a lot of questions about what I was doing and were very eager to talk about what was going on in their own lives.

My girlfriend had just given birth to our baby. Suddenly I had a daughter and started thinking about things like what it means to be a parent. And the kinds of things that kids need when they're growing up. I'll be honest with you. I had been a pretty heavy drinker and had had problems with drugs. But now I wanted to start changing my life. I started cleaning up my act, you could say. I became very involved in a lot of physical exercise—kind of like my own rehab program—and I stopped the drinking and the drugs. I spent a lot of time playing basketball and doing other sports. And that's when the neighborhood kids started noticing me and coming up to me to talk.

I'm not really sure why they picked me, but people say I'm a good listener. I listened to their questions, and I would talk with them and try to answer them. First they would start asking me if I could show them different sport moves. Then they would ask me to come to their school, and I would say yes. Sometimes it seemed like they were shocked or stunned by my response. These kids didn't have a whole lot of people paying attention to them. If they were having problems at school—with a teacher, for instance—there was no one to go to school for them; their parents were having a lot of problems of their own.

So I would go and talk with some of the teachers and try to explain the kinds of pressures these kids were under. Then I'd go back to the kids and relate to them what they were doing wrong. And they needed that, because a lot of their parents didn't even care if they went to school.

After a while, I was spending 20 or 30 hours a week with these kids, going to the schools, playing ball with them, and just basically hanging out and talking. The children I was involved with—kind of an informal group of about 20 or 30 children, ranged in age from about five to 17 or 18. We would hang out together, playing ball. But the neighborhood was pretty dangerous. You could get hit with a stray bullet just playing basketball in the park. So I started taking the kids on trips outside the neighborhood.

Ruth: Our group, the Visitacion Valley Parents for Youth, saw what Brian was doing with those kids. He was beginning to turn some of them around. As a preschool teacher, I've been involved with children for years. I've seen how not having a father around can affect them. I've seen this with my own son. So I tried to encourage Brian and help him, as much as I could.

Our group didn't have much money, but people gave what they had, and I managed to get a personal loan so

161

that we could purchase a van for Brian to take the children on trips around the city.

Brian: Most of these kids had never been out of the neighborhood. What they see here is what they think life is all about. "Hey," I told them, "there's a whole world outside of Visitacion Valley." So we would pile into the van, and my mother and some other adults would sometimes come along to help supervise, and we'd just take off. We would go to parks and malls, and I would take them to bookstores. Nobody ever took these kids to the public library, so they thought I was crazy when I told them we were going to a bookstore. "Hey, man," they would say, "why are we going to a bookstore?" But when we got there—to one of those superstores—they had never seen so many books. And for some of them, it opened their eyes. I bought them a few books, and they became excited. You see, with these kids, no one ever bought them a book before.

Ruth: Brian's right. He and I had set up a kind of makeshift library for the neighborhood kids in our basement. We bought the books ourselves, and people contributed what they could. But the books weren't theirs. And it's just not the same.

Brian: I would also take the kids to play basketball in other neighborhoods, with other neighborhood teams, and act as coach. Sometimes, if it was a rough area, there might be trouble. So I started to talk with them about how to avoid trouble; how not to be provoked. And they would listen. I guess because in the past, I've had my own share of trouble. These kids knew that, and they saw me pull myself together. "If I could do it," I would tell them, "you can do it, too."

Ruth: We've been involved with dozens and dozens of

youngsters over the years. Each one is unique, of course, but they were all struggling with the same kinds of problems. Daryl Smith* is a good example of what I'm talking about. I've known him since he was two years old, when he came to the preschool program I was running. There was no father, and his mother was in and out of jail. He was being raised by his grandmother, but she was kind of old and didn't really know how to relate to kids.

Right from the beginning, Daryl was one of the angriest children I ever saw. He had an explosive temper, even then.

Brian: When Daryl was about five years old, he started coming down to the basketball practices I was running. It was hard for him to interact with the other kids—his temper was always on a hair trigger—but he'd talk with me. I'd listen and talk with him about trying to handle the angry feelings he was carrying around with him. From the first, I tried to help him use sports as an outlet for those feelings. And he was a good athlete.

He was making some progress, starting to get along with the other kids better, but there were problems when he began going to school. He was stubborn. The teachers would get on his case, and he would explode in the classroom. He had no one to go to school for him, to see if things could be worked out. So I went. They just couldn't control him in class, and so the school decided, when he was about nine years old, to put him in a special-education class. You know, the kinds of classes they put kids in who have learning disabilities, or are maybe a little retarded. Well, Daryl wasn't either of those things. He knew the

*pseudonym

kinds of kids that were in those classes, and to him it was like saying the school was just giving up on him, that they thought he wasn't good enough to be in a regular class.

Ruth: Finally, I got Daryl into a program that's run by the Police Officers' Association, a kind of recreational and mentor program. But a lot of kids in the program had been in trouble with the law, and some were still involved with drugs. Daryl's mother was an addict, and all his life he had seen what it had done to her. He hated the drug users and dealers.

Sometimes he'd provoke these kids and basically inform on the other kids to the policemen in the program. The police began to be worried for his safety—they were concerned there might be some kind of retaliation. So pretty soon Daryl was out of the program. It seemed, for a while, there wasn't a place on earth for this child.

Brian: But despite everything, he kept coming to the practices. He'd never miss. I kept talking to him and trying to encourage him. It didn't work magic, but I think it helped. That and the time he spent at our house. Sometimes there'd be other kids there, sometimes he'd just sit and talk with my mother. It wasn't exactly home for him, but it was something. I'd just keep telling him that we were behind him, that we knew he could get through this and make something of himself. There are so many children in this community who just get lost in the streets. We were worried that would happen to Daryl. But thank God he was never on drugs, and he was good at sports. And being on Brian's team got him out of the neighborhood, on different trips. He saw there was a whole other world out there.

He seemed to be hanging on, but, of course, there were

so many troubled feelings he was carrying inside him. Finally, he had a brush with the law when he was about 14, and we used that incident to finally get him some professional help. He was put in a group home with good counseling services.

It was a rocky road there for him. He would run away and show up at our doorstep. But we would make sure we got him back to the home. The counseling seemed to be working. All those bottled-up feelings started coming out. At one point—-I remember this vividly—-he was talking about his family and just broke down and cried. He cried until it seemed his heart would break, and Brian held him the whole time.

That was the beginning of him turning his life around. He's been doing well the last couple of years. He's planning to go to college—the first one in his family—and hoping to get a sports scholarship. Brian's going to try to help with that.

Brian: Yeah, he seems to be on the right track now. There've been no more problems with the law. I'm betting he's going to make it.

◆

Ruth: While Brian was working with the children and pulling himself together, our little organization kept trying to do what we could. We had tried and tried to get more police assigned to the area, but we weren't having much luck. So the drug dealing and the shooting continued pretty much as before.

I decided we had to take a more aggressive role ourselves, so we began to confront the dealers directly. We weren't trying to be social workers and get them to give up dealing. But we wanted them to stay away from certain places in the neighborhood and especially from the young kids. There was more than one time that I spoke to these dealers myself. People said I was crazy to do that. But you know, they never touched me, not once.

With small grants from the community's Unitarian Church, the mayor's office, and an organization in Berkeley called Common Counsel, we were able to take the kids throughout the Bay Area and to Los Angeles and Fresno. Brian and I saved up and took a bunch of kids to a dude ranch once. They loved seeing the horses. Up until that time, they had only seen horses in the movies or on TV.

And Brian began to be asked to do some speaking and coaching at the neighborhood schools.

Brian: Yeah, I go and talk about some of the activities we do, and ask them to become involved. It's not just trips and playing basketball. We have these kids do things to help the community. For instance, several times a year we organize a major cleanup at our town park. The local businesses provide the food and the equipment, and the kids work on the grounds. I've also taken them with me to help the neighborhood seniors; when furniture has to be moved or there are other chores, they can't manage on their own.

Ruth: Brian and I, and our neighborhood group, are trying our best to do what we can. I used to run a day-care center here in our home, before I hurt my back. And so we're used to having children around constantly. Hardly a day goes by that kids aren't knocking on the door asking for Brian, or asking me for money or ice cream or some little treat. Sometimes they come to us with good news to share. But a lot of times the news is bad. This community has so many problems. There always seems to be a child or two staying here temporarily when things are bad at home. But, a little at a time, I think we're starting to make some progress.

Brian and Ruth have received a number of awards for their work, including community-service awards from the California Legislative Assembly and the U.S. Congress, but as of this writing they continue to refuse traditional government funding for their actions. They just don't want to deal with the bureaucracy and red tape, they say. They'd rather do things their way.

CREATING A LITTLE PIECE OF HEAVEN: NEW YORK, NEW YORK

Edwin Santos lives on New York City's lower East Side, where every street has too many empty lots filled with rubble, trash, and drug dealers. When he was nine years old, Edwin joined older neighbors in reclaiming one such empty lot. They started by carting away load after load of garbage and rubble, then planting a few plants. Over time, with lots of hard work and donated greenery, they created one of the liveliest community gardens in New York. Edwin, who will be 23 this year, has spent countless hours discouraging dealers from doing business near the garden and helping kids learn to garden—"something better to do than hang out." Although Edwin is now in college part-time, he serves on the garden's board of directors and has an official, paid position overseeing its activities.

This particular community garden is about 150 feet by 75 feet. Visitors enter it through a black wrought-iron gate. In the middle of the garden stands a gazebo, painted antique white, with carved moldings. Never once has it been marred by graffiti, in contrast to the buildings that surround the garden. Visitors notice, to their right, more than 30 garden plots, which yield an abundance of vegetables and fruits. Some of these plots belong to individuals or groups who donate money to the garden. Others are plots for the community at large; they require no donation.

To the left is a stage where music, dance, and other performances take place. Flowers bloom throughout the garden, and benches invite visitors to sit and enjoy the environment. For children, there is a special playing field and workshops in visual arts, crafts, and theater. There is even a 4-H club. During the summer, Edwin takes interested youngsters to museums and other parts of the city, introducing them to new places, ideas, and art.

There are rules in this special place, and they are strictly enforced: no drinking, no drugs, no loud music. The eight-member governing board, started by Edwin and Norman Vallea, the garden's founder, is community-based; they are responsible for creating and implementing garden policy. Interestingly, the drug dealers, gangs, and vandals so prevalent in this part of the city have left the garden alone. Other problems that plague the neighborhood have not appeared here. Residents have an unspoken agreement: The garden and what it symbolizes will be protected by all segments of the community.

Edwin can barely remember a time when creating and nurturing the garden weren't a part of his life. "It was my friend Norman who was my true inspiration," says Edwin. "He created this garden and helped me see why it was so important."

As a child, growing up with a single mother and two siblings, Edwin sometimes found the neighborhood he lived in frightening. Drug dealers and addicts were a regular fixture on lower East Side streets. One day Edwin was walking near his home when he spotted a man trying to clean up rubble in an empty lot adjacent to an abandoned building. A strapping New Englander, Norman was a former construction worker who had been disabled in a work-related accident. He lived in the neighborhood and day after day saw young children playing in the dirty, refuse-filled empty lots. They had nowhere else to go.

Though he was in pain from his disability, Norman was determined to reclaim one of those lots for his young neighbors. Edwin described his friend and his work with the garden in a recent interview.

> You see, Norman was a Buddhist. He believed that if you do good, it will eventually come back to you. He treated everybody with kindness—kids and adults.
>
> When he got this idea, to make a garden out of that abandoned lot, he wasn't expecting people to pitch in. He was going to do it all himself. But then one day I was passing by and saw him working. We started to talk, and he asked me if I'd like to help him. I said sure. Soon other kids from the neighborhood got involved, and some adults

as well. We started to cart off load after load of rubble and began planting some plants. We were all beginning to get excited about what we were doing.

But then the drug dealers started to get angry. That lot was one of their favorite hangouts. They didn't want to give it up at first. So Norman spoke with them. He explained what he was trying to do, and why it was so important to the kids in the neighborhood. And believe it or not, they backed down. They found another place to go. I asked Norman, "Were you scared?" He just shrugged, but I think he must have been scared, at least a little bit.

Norman taught me a lot about courage, and about the importance of treating people fairly. Everyone trusted him. I spent a lot of time with him, when he was teaching me how to garden and how to care about the environment. That was okay with my mom, who was very protective, because she trusted him, too. He used to come to our house on holidays, like Thanksgiving, and he would invite us and a lot of the neighbors for potluck suppers at his place.

He encouraged a lot of kids in the neighborhood to develop their talents, especially in art. He and his friend Renaldo helped organize some neighborhood programs that helped kids learn to draw. I'm making sure that those programs continue today.

Norman believed that life was sacred. And that we all have a responsibility to help other people. But he could be a pretty shrewd negotiator, too, if it was something he believed in. That's how he got a lot of donations from organizations and different people to help us. I hope I've learned that from him.

I remember, one time, Steven Spielberg was shooting a

film right down the block. I guess he wanted to set a certain mood. Anyway, the garden was a problem for the film crew. It didn't make the neighborhood look bleak enough. They spoke to Norman and offered him a lot of money to tear the garden down. Of course he refused. But they worked out some kind of a deal, so that Norman covered the plants with blankets and trimmed some of the hedges. And the garden was saved. Steven Spielberg was so impressed with Norman that he donated the money for the garden's gazebo and the wrought-iron gate that we now have.

Norman made sure that everything in the garden was wheelchair-accessible. He was always thinking of others. The marble slate that's in the garden, Norman carried that piece by piece from old, abandoned buildings around town. He wanted the people who live here to be able to look at things of beauty. He encouraged kids to follow their dreams, and he helped them believe that they could do that. He wanted to keep them away from the drug dealers, like he did with me. Now I feel an obligation to do all that with other kids. So I go into the schools in my area and talk with students in the elementary grades about what we do in the garden. It's a way of helping themselves, I tell them, and a way of helping the whole community.

It's hard, sometimes, to excite kids about gardening, or doing something for the environment. Especially when some of them have never been out to the country, or even to a place like Central Park.

But I try my best to reach them, because the alternative is life on the streets. I tell them about what it meant to me, to help create this place. And I tell them about the happiness the garden gives to people. I say, "You can do that. You can help make people happy, and have some fun, too."

Some kids decide to check it out. And mostly they like it when they come. We usually find things for them to do that interests them. They like feeling that they can be useful and be a part of something like this—even the so-called "tough-guys" who won't admit it. They may grumble, but they keep coming back. And if they don't come back, well, at least we tried. And we keep on trying. I'm stubborn. I don't like to give up on kids. I keep thinking how I might have turned out if there hadn't been a Norman or a garden. Other kids deserve the same chance that I had. That's why Norman and I kept bugging the schools and the other community groups to back us up. A lot of schools in the area have begun sending their students to the garden for community-service projects.

The garden's thriving now, and bursting with activities. But Norman's gone. In 1994, his health finally gave out and he died. I was pretty upset. I would sit in the garden, with everything in bloom, and feel such life around me; it was hard to believe that the person who started it all was dead. But then I began to see that Norman's still with us, in a way, because the garden continues to live and to grow. It's what he would want, and it's what I want, and a whole new generation of kids want it, too.

LESSONS FROM HISTORY: CLIFTON, NEW JERSEY

In the fall of 1988, in the sleepy little town of Clifton, New Jersey, adolescents from some of the town's most respected families committed acts of vandalism against Jewish establishments around town. Citizens were unsure how to respond. Should the perpetrators be punished? Would these youths respond to rehabilitation? One man, Rabbi Eugene Markovitz, was convinced he had the answer. In an April 1995 interview, he related the story.

It happened on Halloween Eve of 1988. The morning after, my wife and I discovered that our garage door was painted over with swastikas, four-letter words, and all kinds of nasty remarks, such as: "We hate Jews"; "Hitler should have killed you all"; "Go back to your own country." You know the sort of thing I'm talking about.

We soon found out that the same thing had been done at the Clifton Jewish Center, at a kosher butcher store a few blocks away, and at the home of a Jewish family in our neighborhood. Four places.

As you can imagine, everybody was very hurt and indignant about this. My neighbors and everybody else. But it did not take long—three or four weeks—before the vandals were apprehended. They were a bunch of teenagers, and they had boasted to their friends. So they got caught.

Before the Juvenile Court hearing, the judge called me to ask my opinion about what he should do with them. These boys were the 14, 15 years old. Four of them were involved. They were the children of very prominent families. One of them was the son of a dentist, one a banker's son, a teacher's son, and so on.

I did a lot of thinking about what I should tell the judge. It struck me that these kids had done what they did during the week of the 50th anniversary of

Kristallnacht, the night of the broken glass. As you may remember, this was the night the Nazis went on a rampage throughout Germany, burning and looting synagogues, Jewish shops, and businesses. Everybody was talking about this. It was on all the news programs, on television and so forth. Was there some kind of perverse connection between the anniversary of Kristallnacht and these kids' actions? What had caused this kind of hatred? I didn't know, but it troubled me. I couldn't stop thinking about it.

Finally, I wrote a letter to the judge and I said these kids had to make restitution, but I would be opposed to any other kind of punishment right now. I felt we should try something else, and that is to educate. I wanted a chance to educate these kids. In my heart, I felt it was the right thing to do, and I explained my reasoning, at some length, in the letter.

To my surprise, a few days later when these kids and their families appeared in court, the judge read the letter out loud. And he decided to take me up on it. The judge, a very prominent judge and a non-Jew, had been deeply upset by all this and had felt that a strong example should be set to show that the community was not going to tolerate this kind of behavior. He was ready to send these boys to reform school. But he decided to accept my suggestion. He ruled that the boys had to make restitution, to perform 30 hours of community service and attend 25 hours of instruction with me. They were ordered to be at my disposal whenever I wanted to meet with them.

Well, to tell you the truth, I wasn't exactly sure what I was going to do with these boys. How could I reach them? I had never done anything like this before. My instinct was to try to give them a sense of history so they would understand the seriousness of what they had done.

Bear in mind my background—in addition to being a rabbi, I'm a professor of American history. I have a doctorate in the subject, and I was determined to try to convey a sense of the meaning of America to these boys. But how? I decided, before I started the sessions, to call a meeting of all the boys' parents so we could have a chance to talk with one another. At first there was some tension. Let's face it, if you were a parent, you would not feel terribly comfortable in that situation.

So I said to them, "Look, before I begin my venture with your children I want to get to know you a little bit. I want to know what you think about how this came about. Why would your children, who come from such wonderful homes, do such a thing? What's your theory?" I told them I was not going to ask for volunteers. I would insist that each one of them tell me what they thought.

One of the parents said, "It must have been peer pressure." Another said, "It must be the influence of television." Still another said, "Some programs tend to glorify the swastika as a kind of symbol." They gave all kinds of excuses.

I told them, after they finished, "Haven't we left out one thing: yourself, the family. Do you think that you, maybe your own family, might have had some little role in what your kids did? Maybe you spoke about Jews in a certain way during suppertime; maybe your attitude toward Jews or toward blacks or Hispanics was conducive to your kids' drawing particular conclusions. Is that possible?"

Naturally there was a chorus of "No, no, no, that cannot be." You know, "Our best friends are Jews," that sort of thing.

One of the parents, however, spoke very movingly. He's a man from Holland. He grew up there. He was raised by his grandfather, and they lived in a small town near the sea. His grandfather had a modest house and there was an extra room. In this room, during World War II, he hid a Jewish family from the Nazis. Of course, he knew he could have been arrested or killed, but he did it anyway. He was a good Christian, a pious man. This parent, who was now sitting in my office, had tears in his eyes when he told me how proud he was of his grandfather. "If I live a thousand years," he said, "I will never understand why my son did this, where he got this idea."

"Did you ever tell this story to your children?" I asked. He admitted that he had never talked about this story to any of his kids. To anyone at all, in fact. He wasn't sure why.

Let me tell you, it was very moving. In the end, each of the parents engaged in conversation with me. We parted as friends, I like to think. They wished me well, good luck, and all of that. We agreed that we would meet again, after my sessions with their sons. And we would compare notes.

So here I was, ready to meet with these boys, and I still wasn't sure what I was going to do. I figured that eventually it would come to me. But first, I had to get a sense of who these kids were. At the beginning they were quite antagonistic, I can tell you. They poked fun at yarmulkes, they poked fun at this, they poked fun at that.

When I first started meeting with them, they showed no remorse. And you know what? I didn't ask for any. What good would that do? It would be worth less than zero at that point. They wouldn't even know how to articulate it. Fourteen-, 15-year-old kids; they would give self-serving little answers. I wasn't interested in that. I never even asked them why they did what they did. Not then, anyway.

I decided to take them down to the Jewish Center. I said, "I'm going to take you to the place that you poked fun at; the place you think is so terrible. We'll see what a synagogue looks like, what it's all about."

So we went. They weren't too happy about it, but what could they do? I had, as they say, a captive audience. I started speaking with them about the commonality of religions. I showed them a Bible and opened it up. "Here are the same stories that you read in your church," I told them. Opening up a prayer book, choosing prayers—all of a sudden they showed some signs of recognition. It wasn't so different from what they did in their church. We spent some time talking about this. Well, to be honest, I did most of the talking and they did the listening. Then our first session ended. It was at least a beginning, I thought.

The next time we met, I invited the Catholic bishop of the Paterson diocese, a personal friend of mine, to join us. He's a very important man to these boys. Next to the pope, he's one of the most important men in the church hierarchy, at least in this country. I hadn't told the boys he was going to be there, so they were very surprised, as you can imagine. But I thought, one picture is worth a thousand words. So when they came in for their lesson, there he was. He was wearing a cap, his own pink yarmulke. And I sat next to him, wearing a black yarmulke. The bishop and I kidded around about the yarmulkes. I asked him to talk about why he wears one, and he did. Then he told the boys why the Jews wear yarmulkes. And these kids were really stupefied. It blew their minds (to use one of their phrases). Then the bishop and I exchanged yarmulkes, and we talked about what else our religions have in common. That was the day, I think, they started listening. The next time the boys and I met, I decided to focus on the subject of America. Because, you know, these boys had written on my garage, "Go back to your own country." Well, I came to this country in 1940 from Romania, when I was 19 years old. This has been my country for over 50 years. These kids had no idea what this country means to me or, for that matter, what it meant to them. They thought that God had just plunked them down here.

I said to them, "Tell me about the people in your family who first came to America. How did they get here?" Well, you know what? They didn't know. They didn't have a clue. So I sent them back to their families and told them to find out. And they did. They brought back all kinds of stories. They really got into it. It was a revelation to them that they had all come from Europe—not so very far from where I came from. You see, they had no real sense of who they were, where they had come from, and why their ancestors had wanted to come to America.

Then we got on the subject of prejudice in America. Now they were starting to realize that their relatives from generations ago had experienced prejudice, too. I asked them to read a newspaper—any newspaper—and to bring me back examples of words and phrases that seemed to them to be prejudiced, or stories about people being hurt or victimized because of their religion or the color of their skin. Well, they looked and they found, as I knew they would.

They came back with examples, and we talked about them. At this point I started to see some changes in them. I thought they might be ready to start learning about the Holocaust. So I showed them a French documentary. This was before *Schindler's List* came out. And let me tell you, it was shock treatment for these boys. They couldn't believe what they were seeing with their own eyes.

But the enormity of the Holocaust was hard for them to grasp. I could understand that, so I tried to make it more personal. I paired each one of the boys with a victim of the Nazis who was about his age. Not just Jews, mind you. As we all know, Jews weren't the only victims. The boys' job was to find out what happened to these other kids. Of course I helped them, told them where to look.

They came back the next week with the information. They were pretty shaken up. They had done their homework, and what they had found was not a pretty story. It was very hard for them to accept. They felt outrage and sadness. You could see it in their eyes.

It was then that they told me they wanted to erase what they had painted on my garage door. You see, up until that time I had never permitted the graffiti to be cleaned up. On the synagogue, on the other places they had painted the slurs, they cleaned up everything. My garage door was a different story. I wanted them to be confronted by what they had done each time they passed my house. In the beginning, they hadn't understood the meaning of their actions. They didn't know how it affected those of us who were the targets. Now they were beginning to grasp it. And it hurt them. But still, I was noncommittal.

Not long after that session they showed up at my house, all on their own, with soap and water, and cleaned up everything they had painted on my garage. That was seven or eight years ago, and they're doing fine now, every one of them. Never got in trouble again.

Well, let's face it, I was lucky. Some kids you can't reach no matter what you do. But these kids, they were decent boys. They just needed some help. A lot of kids don't have that. Education was the key here. I believe that when a child is born, he's neither good nor bad. He is born, as they say, with a "clean slate." It's what we write on the minds and the hearts of a child that's the important thing. I believe that up to a certain age, no matter what the problem, a child can be reached. Anyway, we have to try. To give up on a child is a terrible thing. In Judaism, it's literally a sin to give up on a child.

Here we had a group of boys who knew nothing about religion. Never mind Judaism, they knew nothing about any religion. They knew nothing about the Holocaust, they had no idea of the kind of impact a swastika would have on a Jew, or the word "nigger" on an African-American.

I was struck by the fact that these kids were so ignorant of what America is all about. After all, America means freedom. It means having respect for somebody else's feelings and beliefs and trying to get along and working together with all kinds of people—no matter who they are or where they come from. If that's not the meaning of America, what is?

In my opinion, most Americans are decent. There is a fundamental decency in this country—don't let anyone tell you otherwise. I see it wherever I go. I'll give you an example. I was on a radio program, talking about what I did with these boys, and a black woman called up and said, "Rabbi, God bless you and the work you're doing. If only you were there when my son got into trouble."

Her son did some damage or mischief in a park. And he got caught and thrown into jail, and then went to some kind of reform school. It was rough. The other kids beat him up and tormented him. He came out of this experience very bitter and full of anger.

"And nobody cared!" this mother told me. "If only someone like you had been there when this happened to my son."

Since the incident described above, Rabbi Markovitz has been asked to speak about his ideas to organizations around the country. His message of responding to young people who commit hate crimes with education instead of punishment has struck a responsive chord among jurists, educators, clergy, and parents.

Chapter Five
EXCEPTIONAL CHILDREN...
EXCEPTIONAL PARENTS

What is it that makes some children unusually empathic and caring toward others? Are they born that way? Have certain life experiences brought out those traits? Or is it the way they were raised by their parents?

The Giraffe Project is an organization that seeks out and honors adults and children who have "stuck their necks out" for the common good. For more than 10 years, the Project has kept meticulous records, now numbering in the hundreds, that profile these special people. Going through these files, I came across case after case of youngsters who did some extraordinary things.

There was eight-year-old James Ale, for example, of Davie, Florida. In 1985, his friend was hit by a car while playing in the street because there was no playground nearby. Upon hearing that his friend had been hurt, James got on the phone to the local media, telling them that his neighborhood desperately needed a park for children to play in. Month after month, he campaigned for the "children of Davie," making phone calls and writing letters to city officials. At one point, he showed up at the mayor's office with a briefcase and a typed letter signed "James Ale for the Children of Davie." His efforts finally paid off: A year and a half later, a new city park was opened.

I also read about 11-year-old Ashley Black of Freehold, New Jersey. In 1991, she saw a television news story about European computer games. Manufacturers in Austria and Germany were making Nazi theme games with titles such as "Aryan Test," in which players earned points for gassing or hanging death-camp prisoners often identified as Jews or "Polaks." Ashley was so upset that she started a petition campaign to have the games banned in her state. Within two months, she had collected more than 2,000 signatures. She enlisted other children in her cause and helped to mobilize the local media. Her actions helped create an international agreement stating that Austria and Germany will not export any of these games to the U.S.

Then there was Kanésha Sonée Johnson. In 1994, she started fifth grade in Hawthorne, California. She saw that the Vietnamese and African-American kids in her class kept to themselves, often taunting children from other cultures. Kanésha, an African-American, thought that was wrong, so she began making friends with Vietnamese youngsters who couldn't speak English, helping them with their homework, teaching them the ropes, and telling other kids to "lay off." Kanésha was called a lot of names herself but she held her ground, even ending de facto segregation on the playground. After seeing African-

Americans and Asians choose only each other for their teams, Kanésha managed to persuade the children to play together. Because of her efforts, all the school's teams are now integrated.

It's impossible to read these stories, and others like them, without pondering how these children developed into the kind of youngsters they are. Was there some crucial common denominator?

After I investigated further and spoke with some of these children's families, it seemed clear to me that the answer is yes. There is one common denominator that I found in virtually every case: Each child had parents or other crucial role models who either taught them the importance of compassion and courage by example or unequivocally supported the children's own determined instincts to right a wrong or respond to people who needed help. These kids believed they could make a difference, and their parents believed that, too. That very belief— however impractical and "pie-in-the-sky" it may have seemed to others—is what helped these children to achieve what they did against all expectations.

The following profiles, derived in part from material provided by the Giraffe Project and in part from interviews with the children's parents, describe children and parents who were not initially extraordinary in any way. They were not endowed with unusual intellectual or artistic gifts. They were not living through dramatic, extraordinary times, and they were not privileged with great wealth. They were essentially "average" except in one respect: The parents of these children—whether by instinct, education, or personal beliefs—practiced the principles that research has shown to be vital in raising compassionate, courageous children. These parents hadn't talked with any researchers or read about these lessons. Instead, they simply lived them.

BRIANNE SCHWANTES

Brianne Schwantes attracted national attention when she turned up as a volunteer during the 1993 floods. It wasn't just that she was 13. Brianne has a rare disease that makes her bones break at the slightest pressure. Nevertheless, she was determined to assist flood victims and spent long hours in Iowa helping with the cleanup and inspiring other volunteers. When floods hit Georgia in 1994, Brianne hit the phones to organize another relief team that she and her family joined.

Not so well known is Brianne's role as a pioneer and champion for other kids with *osteogenesis imperfecta*. "OI" makes bones so brittle that they break even before birth; Brianne was born with more than a dozen breaks. She's been a research subject at the National Institutes of Health all of her 15 years, as NIH looks for ways in which kids with OI can enrich their lives. Brianne thinks her own life has been enriched by being active rather than living on pillows. Brianne calls herself "a guinea pig, because if the doctors are going to try something new, they try it on me first." She takes the responsibility seriously, hoping her experience will help other kids with OI. She publishes a newsletter for them, reporting on research and her own medical experiences as well as sharing stories, book reviews, tips and jokes, and answering letters.

Brianne's mother, Terry Schwantes, remembers that the family was always involved in community projects. They tried to focus on what they had rather than on what they didn't have. Whatever the problems they struggled with, they saw from their community work that other people often had it harder: "Sometimes being in a terrible situation brings out the kindness in other people, and we have learned that helping does make a difference. When my girls were little, I would read them this great biography series where each person represented a virtue or value. For example, Harriet Tubman would represent courage. I felt that reading the kids biographies was important because these were true stories and very good examples for the girls to think about.

"We tried to have everything as normal as possible in terms of our family life. I was always open to suggestions and advice. But I believed in discipline and personal responsibility. I must have said 'put the covers on your magic markers' a thousand times, so the girls always put the covers on their markers. I don't know why that mattered to me, but it did.

"Brianne spent lots of time around kids who were ill and staying at the Ronald McDonald house. She met kids with all kinds of diseases and disabilities, including kids with AIDS. She saw that everyone had fears, but she also saw a lot of kindness. Brianne doesn't judge people. She takes them as they are. That's a hard thing to do. But it's important.

"I don't think there's some kind of 'empathy gene.' Kids aren't born with it. It has to be taught. People always assume that other people will be doing the good deeds, but that may not be true. We can't count on that. So sensitizing kids has to start when they are very young.

"It hasn't been easy for us. I had to go away a lot with Brianne, and it was very hard on my younger daughter, Elizabeth. One day, when she was upset, I burst into tears and told her it was hard on me, too. She needed to hear me say that. She needed to realize that she was not the only one hurting. It would not have helped to try to shield her. Children need to know that we all hurt.

"I think that listening to your kids is very important. It's a hard world out there, and they need to talk about it. There's so much violence. It's all over the media. When there's something violent or mean-spirited on TV, my girls and I talk about it. That helps, but it doesn't take away all their fears. With all that Brianne has done and contributed, it makes me mad that she is afraid to go out at night. So is her sister. They fear they might be attacked or killed. Kids can't take walks like they used to. They have to get rides. I feel bad about that. I wish it were different."

TREVOR FERRELL

One cold December night in 1983, 11-year-old Trevor Ferrell saw a news story on television that upset him. It showed homeless people sleeping on the streets in nearby Philadelphia, bundled up in all the clothes they owned. Trevor was afraid the people would freeze to death. He went into action. Grabbing a blanket and his special pillow, he asked his parents to drive him into the city so he could give the bedding to a needy person. His mother thought the city streets were too dangerous at night, but his dad thought the experience might teach Trevor to appreciate his own comfortable life.

The Ferrells piled into the family station wagon and drove 12 miles to downtown Philadelphia. Trevor held the blanket under the car heater to warm it up. As they cruised the dark city streets, he spotted a shoeless man lying atop a grate. With his father standing nearby, Trevor approached the stranger and politely offered him the blanket. The homeless man was startled at first by such kindness, then burst into a smile. "Thank you, and God bless you," he said to the boy.

This made Trevor feel so good that he and his mother dug out two blankets to give away the next night. His parents told him that his reward for any night he finished all his homework would be a run downtown to distribute blankets and warm clothing. The Ferrell family soon knew many of the homeless people by name. They realized that the street people were not just cold, they were also hungry, so they started making sandwiches and soup and coffee to hand out, too.

The Ferrell station wagon became a familiar sight on the city streets. One winter night a letter was left in their car that said: "Last night in my loneliness, poverty, and utter despair I could have ended it all. It was freezing cold and pouring rain . . . . Suddenly in front of me stood a little boy with a face of spring, who gave me a respectful, 'Here, sir, I have a blanket for you.' He had given me more than a blanket; he gave me new hope. I could not keep back tears. I fell in love with the little boy named Trevor, and at the same time I fell in love again with life."

By this time the Ferrells were running out of spare clothing and blankets, so Trevor wrote signs for his church and his dad's store, asking for donations for the homeless. When the local newspaper covered "Trevor's Campaign," the publicity brought a flood of donated food, clothes, blankets, and, most important, volunteers. TV and magazine reporters picked up the story of the young boy who cared so much for the people on the streets.

When some schoolmates made fun of his campaign and the media attention that he was getting, Trevor took them along on the nightly food run. Three of them became new volunteers.

With so much community interest, Trevor's Campaign was able to grow beyond the nightly food and clothing route. Within a year, Trevor's Place, a shelter where homeless people could stay while they looked for homes and jobs, opened its doors. Next came a thrift store to raise money for the project, and then Next Door, a residence and training center for single mothers and their families. Today Trevor's Campaign serves more than 200 people a day; 15 cities across the country have set up branches.

His father runs Trevor's Campaign now, but Trevor comes home on weekends to work at the shelters or drive one of the three food vans on the nightly runs. He also makes speeches around the country to encourage other students and adults to work with the homeless. Despite all the publicity, he remains dedicated to helping people.

Frank Ferrell vividly remembers the night his son was first inspired to take action: "Trevor was watching TV when he should have been doing his homework. He came running into the kitchen to tell us what he had seen, and we sent him to his room until his homework was finished. But Trevor kept shouting, 'You should see it! People are sleeping on the street in Philadelphia!' We knew that was so, and to be honest we had never thought much about it. We had considered those people 'bums' and had never felt much for them. Anyway, Trevor continued to nag us about this news story. He couldn't stay in his room; he kept insisting that something had to be done for these people. We thought this would be a good opportunity to teach Trevor that everyone doesn't live in the suburbs, with cars and nice houses. And what happened that night was a truly touching experience for all of us. We kept driving back there every night, bringing more gifts. And that is how Trevor's Campaign began.

"It hasn't been easy for Trevor. He was often ridiculed at school by his peers. They called him a goody-goody or 'blanket boy.' But then Trevor had an idea. He decided to take some of these kids on our nightly food run, and they came with us, onto the streets. And believe it or not, it worked. That's how some of them became volunteers themselves.

"I wish I could say I encouraged him to do what he was doing. But Trevor had full confidence that what he was doing was right, and he ended up transforming those kids who teased him.

"Despite the wonderful work Trevor was doing, we had a problem. He was doing very poorly in school and failed sixth grade twice. His dyslexia made school a terrible struggle for him, though he kept trying. We gave him all the support we could. We've always believed in the importance of education. So does Trevor. Even after he was recognized for his homeless project, he turned down a visit with the pope so he would not miss the orientation for a special school for learning-disabled kids. [He did eventually get to meet with the pope, sometime later.]"

When asked if he feels empathy is learned, Mr. Ferrell responds earnestly that he believes kids need to have examples. "Actually, I don't think we were such great examples ourselves, but kids have to have examples somewhere. I think all of us are born with the capacity for empathy, but it gets twisted somewhere along the way. Then we have to relearn it again.

"Frankly, all the publicity that Trevor's actions generated has been very hard on our family. I would often answer the phone 'Hi, I'm Trevor's dad.' Well, I have three other children in addition to Trevor, and they would protest, 'Hey, you're my dad, too!' It was tough."

The Ferrells worry about the messages that kids today are getting. "The media seems to focus so much on what's bad in life," Mr. Ferrell asserts. "It pays too much attention to violence. It's not that I'm a prude—I just don't think it's right. No matter how bad things get, there is always a group somewhere doing what is right and good, and that's what keeps the planet going."

"Trevor was always a compassionate kid," Janet Ferrell joins in. "Even in nursery school, when his speech was bad because of the dyslexia, he was still nice to people. I don't think we did anything so unusual; it's just the way he was.

"The night we went downtown, our intention was to go that one night. I was petrified—I sat in the locked car with the windows rolled up. When Trevor went over to that man on the sidewalk and covered him with his yellow blanket, it was really quite a sight. The man was so kind and appreciative. He knew Trevor was not there to judge him, he was there to help. We had meant to go to Philadelphia just that one night, but we found that we had to keep coming back.

"I thought Trevor was crazy—insane—to want to do this. Now I work with him in the thrift store, which is in a terrible, drug-infested area. There are shootings and violence, and my friends think I'm crazy to be there. But I like it. The people we deal with are so real.

"Trevor is just a normal kid, and we were weird enough to go along with him on his vision. Our other kids share that vision. Trevor's brother Alan once raised $400 for his school so that he and the other kids could have a better gym. Not long after, he and Trevor went down to Haiti to help build houses for the people there, through a church organization.

"Sometimes it can all be a bit overwhelming. Once my daughter asked my husband to go feed the ducks with her at our local duck pond. My husband said, 'No way!' He was afraid that would turn into his next mission in life."

ANDREW HOLLEMAN

Years ago, when Andrew Holleman was 12, his parents received a letter from a local developer inviting them to a meeting to review his construction plans for the wetland area in their town. Having played in the wetland for years, Andrew knew it was full of rare flora and fauna and was much too wet for such a development. Andrew headed for the library and researched the town's master plan, as well as relevant environmental laws, looking for ways to save the wetland. Duly armed, he went door-to-door, urging people to come to the hearing. So many people came that the meeting had to be moved to a bigger hall. There, as a neighbor said, "That kid really took that developer on."

Mobilized town residents formed the Concord Road Neighborhood Council, which raised $16,000 for an attorney and an environmental consultant. For the next seven months, Andrew circulated petitions, talked to the media, raised money, wrote to legislators, and attended all 35 evening town meetings. (He also managed to stay on the honor roll at school.) In the spring, scientific testing was done, proving Andrew's contention that the site could not support the sewage system for such development. The proposal was denied, and the door was closed on any similar proposals in the future.

Andrew is now trying to get state funding to buy the property and turn it into a nature preserve. He is the youngest recipient of both the United Nations' Global 500 Award and the Environmental Protection Agency's 1988 Regional Merit Award. Andrew's letter to future generations, placed in a "time capsule of hope" buried in Mexico City in June 1995 for the UN's World Environment Day, concluded: "It is our job to save the Earth and if we succeed, it is your job to preserve it."

"I believe that compassion is taught, probably by example," says Cheryl Holleman, Andrew's mother.

"Children learn it when their parents show them love and respect. No one gives compassion unless they get compassion. We hugged our kids a lot. We would have family discussions when everyone expressed their opinions. This taught the kids that we were interested in listening to them, so they continued to listen to us.

"We had regular family conferences to talk about good and bad things. We tried to keep things calm and even. We would say cleaning your room is your responsibility, so let's all clean up. Then, in the same meeting, we might plan a day trip. If you just yell at kids, they will never hear you.

"We aren't activists, but we do act on behalf of our children. We are in awe of Andrew and the results of what he did. Not to mention all the honors and attention he's received. The project he took on grew so fast that sometimes he would get tired and overwhelmed. But we stuck by him. Andrew has a sister, Elizabeth, 16½ months younger than he is, and a brother, Nick, five years younger. The siblings got caught up in all the excitement. They would tell all their friends that Andrew was going to be on TV. Elizabeth would tell people in the supermarket to make sure and use paper, not plastic. I think the kids learned a lot.

"Andrew was humble the whole time he was getting so much attention. This made it easier on the siblings—he really showed no negative behavior at all, and he included his brother and sister whenever possible. Andrew is sensitive about a lot of things. He loves that quote: 'If you are not part of the solution, you are part of the problem.'

"What would I say to other parents? Loving your children in the most important thing, and setting an example. If you have a violent home and you yell and hit—that is what your children will learn. If Mommy and Daddy share, care, and respect each other, then that is what the children will learn.

"Sometimes if a friend was sick, we would bring a little gift. If our elderly friend across the street needed help, we would shovel her walk. You can't sit your kids down for a compassion lesson. It's a long, slow process of showing them. Eventually they will learn by observing you.

"I also think religion helps, any religion, and belief in God. Following the Ten Commandments gives children an important moral framework. One fall the children from our church planted seeds on the side of the church building, and then went back to the site that spring to see what God had created through their hands. It was a wonderful lesson.

"When my kids were young, I worked as an RN while they were in school. But I think it's important to be home when they are home. I would tell my kids to use me as an excuse if they were being pressured by the other kids to do things they didn't want to do or go places they didn't want to go. 'Tell your friends your mom wants you home,' I would say. That helped them stay out of trouble.

"We are so lucky. I know other parents who did their best and their kids still fool around with drugs. There is no guarantee in life how your children will turn out. But there's a lot we can do, with God's help. Then you just pray for the best."

SARAH ACHESON

Sarah Acheson considers herself to be a typical 14-year-old. She likes dancing, shopping, hiking, and talking on the phone. Her days are filled with classes, sports, and homework. But how many typical 14-year-olds have been volunteering at an AIDS hospice for six years?

When she was eight, Sarah visited the hospice that had opened across the street from her school and immediately donated the dollar allowance in her pocket. She's been coming back ever since, bringing drawings, handmade cards, and the proceeds from her lemonade stand. Back at her school, she's gotten kids and adults involved in making drawings for the hospice walls and in baking cookies for the residents.

Most of the patients she's made friends with have died, and some kids have given her a hard time about her atypical interest in the hospice, but Sarah is undaunted. "If I ever got AIDS, I'd want children to care about me, to draw me pictures," Sarah says. "I just figured that's how they felt, too."

Lexine Acheson describes her daughter as the sort of person who is always rooting for the underdog. "She has a natural capacity to care." Growing up, Sarah was exposed to many examples of giving. Mrs. Acheson's sister lived with the family during hard times. Her brother, too, stayed with them for a while, when he was in need. The Achesons were very active in church projects and community-service work. Their home was often the meeting place for other volunteers. "I think children learn by example," says Mrs. Acheson. "They need to see people living out good values. That's how they develop compassion."

After Sarah started her volunteer work, the Achesons separated and then divorced. Sarah has maintained a close relationship with both of her parents. She sees her father regularly and receives continuing encouragement from him and his "significant other." Mr. Acheson leads a group for adult children of alcoholics, as well as many church-related retreats.

Mrs. Acheson describes her daughter as a normal teenager, with her own style and her own dyed hair. Though Sarah and her siblings are involved in many activities, Mrs. Acheson makes sure the family has two weeks of uninterrupted togetherness during the summer. This past summer, they helped lead a Scout group on a camping trip. "Scouting is what I use to help keep my kids away from drugs and other bad influences," she says.

Sarah also participates in Search Rescue in her state of Washington. This is a volunteer effort in which young people between the ages of 14 and 18 team up with adults to search for lost hikers or help out during accidents.

Mrs. Acheson says she believes that parents have to choose a few things to focus on when raising children: "I let my kids know from the very beginning that I would never accept lying. They must tell the truth no matter what—no white lies. I always insisted on honesty and encouraged them always to talk to me. Respect for people, especially older people, was another important virtue. Sarah goes to a private Catholic school and has had some problems agreeing with the authorities. I encourage her to deal with her anger and at the same time have 100 percent respect for those she disagrees with. Honesty and respect are most important to me.

"I believe you raise your children till about 14—then hopefully they will know how to say no to things they do not want to do. I'm just crossing my fingers now. My theory is that we all make mistakes, and we have to live with them.

We must teach our children to weigh decisions very carefully and understand that there are consequences to the things they do. Hopefully I have given them the tools to do that.

"Kids today can easily get depressed and overwhelmed by all the problems in the world. I think we have to make a point of helping them deal with feeling depressed because teen suicide is up so much. The media emphasizes all the negative things—some of this is good for kids to know, but not all of it. Too much exposure is not good; it overwhelms them, and kids say, 'We can't help that the world is so awful. How can we do anything that matters?' I tell them, if you extend yourself to someone, it can make a difference. When you challenge a person to give examples of times they have done something to help someone, most people have a hard time not thinking of several positive examples. Cleaning a driveway for a neighbor who can't is a perfect example. These small deeds can make you feel good and balance out all the bad stuff that's happening. I tell my kids there is a lot of value in small deeds."

Sarah is interested in politics and has hopes of being president someday. Mrs. Acheson thinks that even if she doesn't become president, Sarah will probably have a chance at fixing at least one injustice in the world, and that would be just fine. She tries not to discuss politics with her daughter because she wants her to have her own opinions and not lean on her parents for her ideas. Sarah's sister, Molly, who is nine years old and a Brownie, has her own way of doing what she believes is a good deed. She singles out "ugly" people and says something nice to them. She feels that by talking to them and being friendly, she will make them feel better.

"You see, I was obese for almost my whole life," says Mrs. Acheson, "and my children have learned how hurtful it can be to have to deal with cruel comments, which I often had to do. Now I'm a normal size, but I think they will continue to be sensitive to people who look different.

"My son has befriended a fat girl in his class at school, and I'm sure his experience with me has helped him be sensitive to her feelings. He knows she isn't a bad person.

"The main thing is to be consistent. Focus on the little things they can manage—not world peace. That, unfortunately, they just won't get."

JUSTIN LEBO

Like any normal kid, Justin Lebo used to spend all his allowance on movies, video games, and treats. But not any more. For the past nine years, Justin—now 19—has become a one-man bicycle factory. Working summers and weekends to earn money to buy new parts, he's refurbished more than 250 bikes and given them to children who need them.

When Justin was 10 years old, he and his father rebuilt an old bike they had found at a garage sale. Justin enjoyed stripping off the old dirt and paint, replacing the broken and worn parts, and making the bike look like new. He decided to rebuild another and then another.

But what to do with the bikes? Justin took them to the Kilbarchen Orphan Asylum near his home in New Jersey to give to the boys living there. The 20 boys were excited;

now they had three more bikes to take turns on. But Justin knew it was important for kids to have a bicycle of their own. His mother, Sarah Lebo, remembers, "When he saw how much those kids liked the bikes, he told me that he wanted to get one for every boy there by Christmas."

Justin spent the rest of his summer vacation fixing up bicycles. He worked every day, and when school started he worked every weekend. He and his mom scoured thrift stores and garage sales for bikes—it takes from three to six old bikes to make one good new one. Justin added new grips, seats, pedals, and brakes. He gave each one a new paint job and flashy decals.

As Christmas approached, Justin began to worry. He had 15 bikes ready, but he had run out of battered ones to rebuild. A story in the local newspaper brought in so many junkers that Justin reached his goal: Every boy at Kilbarchen had a bike by Christmas. He went on to rebuild bikes for 11 boys at a second home, and for years kept a good supply of spare parts on hand so he could fill requests from needy families.

What motivated Justin to care so much and take action at such a young age? "I won't take any credit," explains his mother. "It's something inside him. He is a compassionate and sensitive person—that's all."

Mrs. Lebo had hoped to have more children after Justin's birth. She was concerned that he was getting too much attention by being an only child, surrounded by doting relatives and an extended family. She didn't want him to grow up to be "spoiled." So she made a special effort to explain to Justin that not everybody had as much as his family did. The family talked about the importance of helping others on a regular basis. Finally, when Justin was five years old, the Lebos matched Justin's savings and bought Christmas gifts for the children at Kilbarchen. The nuns were so thankful and appreciative that they gave Justin and his mother a tour of the asylum, and Justin was able to see the children who spent most of the year there, lacking many of the things that most children take for granted.

The nun told Justin that people remember to give during the holidays but very often forget during the rest of the year. She said the boys missed having money for the ice-cream truck and other treats and toys. Later the nuns wrote a note to Justin, thanking him for his kindness.

"I am ashamed to say I forgot all about it," says Mrs. Lebo. "You know how you tend to get all involved with your own life." But Justin could not forget. In June, when Justin was six years old, he took out the nun's thank-you note and asked his mother if they could bring money to the children for ice cream. Mrs. Lebo agreed. They subsequently visited the home together many times, always bringing treats for the children. Eventually, those treats became bicycles.

The whole Lebo family, which now included Justin's little sister, pitched in to help Justin reach his goal of giving every child at the asylum a bike of his own. Searching through every possible garage sale for old bicycles and parts became a regular family activity. "Our yard became a dumping ground . . . we must have had 100 bikes," recalls Mrs. Lebo.

It was a wonderful Christmas for the 20 boys at the home, and for Justin. He had reached his goal, but his work was not over. Justin continued to rebuild bikes and donate them to other homes, camps, and shelters. He was awarded the

Point of Light Award in 1990 by President Bush for his volunteer efforts and represented the United States in the United Nations summit on children that same year. But this was not his mother's proudest moment. She remembers, instead, a different incident. Justin was contacted by *People* magazine, which wanted to do a feature story on Justin's efforts. After the phone interview, Justin was sent a copy of the story, with a release form to sign. When Justin read what was written, he realized that the story had been dramatized and exaggerated so much that it was no longer true. Justin felt there was enough real excitement in his story as it actually happened, and that it should not be changed. He refused to sign the release form, despite the writer's pleadings. "But this is the way things are done," the writer tried to persuade Justin. "Don't you want your story to be in a national magazine, with a big picture?" Justin was unmoved. The story didn't run. And that was just fine with Justin.

When asked if there are any disadvantages to being "super-empathic," Justin's mother hesitates for a moment and admits that she thinks there are. "If kids have too much empathy, it can be hard on them socially. Of course, if they don't have enough empathy it's hard on everyone else. To be honest, Justin had to endure a lot of teasing about what he was doing from his peers. They chose to criticize him for spending his time helping those boys instead of doing more 'typical' kinds of things, like sports or going to the mall.

"Some of Justin's friends were just plain tired of hearing their own mothers keep telling them things like 'Why can't you be more like Justin Lebo? He's such a good boy!'

"I know it wasn't easy for my son. But he just kept doing what he felt he had to do. It's important to encourage your children to be sensitive. But at the same time, they need to be a little thick-skinned and independent. If that is possible."

KORY JOHNSON

In 1989, 11-year-old Kory Johnson's sister died from heart disease caused by contaminated well water that Kory's mother drank while she was pregnant. Kory quickly put her grief and anger to work, giving up all her out-of-school hours to fight the poisoning of the environment.

Although some of her peers thought she was "weird" and sometimes gave her a difficult time, others joined her campaign. Adult environmentalists have been amazed by her commitment. She has led her whole family into environmental activism and won John Denver's first Windstar Environmental Youth Award. A Greenpeace spokesperson said that the organization agreed to help fight a toxic incinerator in Phoenix because they knew they could count on the Johnsons' involvement. Kory has testified at public hearings against the construction of the incinerator and has taken a lead in demonstrations and in alerting the media to potential environmental hazards.

A group Kory founded, Children for a Safe Environment (CSE), now has more than 150 members, all of whom have promised to recycle, keep a healthy mind and body, and "never, ever use Styrofoam." A CSE recycling center is thriving in Kory's backyard. CSE makes and distributes canvas shopping bags and has raised money to send children to an environmental learning camp. Apart from that, the group has branched out into social action by collecting blankets for the homeless. In her "spare time," Kory is a cub reporter for the local environmental paper, *Bare Essentials*.

Kory's mother, Terri Johnson, is not at all surprised at the direction Kory's life has taken: "I was a single mom, raising two daughters in Maryville, Arizona. My daughter Amy had been born with a heart defect, my own mother developed cancer and died at the age of 55, and then I developed cancer and had to undergo a hysterectomy. Within just a few years, there were 31 cancer deaths in our small community, and we were becoming more and more alarmed. We appealed to the government for help, but nothing was done. Finally, a newspaper reporter from *New Times*, a Phoenix-based paper, and a nun who was the principal of a local school where a number of students had contracted leukemia, spearheaded an investigation. Ultimately it was discovered that the local well water and land had been poisoned by high concentrates of industrial waste.

"In the meantime, Amy was becoming increasingly ill. She was in and out of hospitals and Ronald McDonald houses. The way Kory coped was to act like a little social worker. She was very comfortable around people and often acted like the official 'welcome wagon.' She would show new families where the kitchen was in the hospital, and help out in any way she could. She was very influenced by Amy, who was battling her illness as hard as she could.

"One day Amy saw a man named Henry Lansworth on the *Today* show, talking about how he was providing lodging for kids who were terminally ill and visiting Disney World. He did this through the Give Kids the World program in Florida. He had been one of the people on Schindler's list and had managed to survive the Holocaust. When he came to America, he began working in the hotel business. He worked his way up and finally owned several hotels. Mr. Lansworth wanted to give something back to this country. That was why he started the project.

"Well, my daughter Amy decided she had something to tell this man, and she wrote him a letter. In the letter she told Mr. Lansworth that he should really meet some of the people he was trying to help so he could learn about their special needs. She suggested that the doors be wider for wheelchair access, and that oxygen be available in the rooms, as well as other special supplies. The letter made quite an impression on him. He called me and asked to meet my daughter. He said he was so inspired and moved by her letter that he decided to build an entire village for the children. All because of Amy. He flew our whole family out to Florida to give Amy the key to the city. He planned for her to be the first child to spend the night there."

Sadly, Amy didn't live to see the project completed. On Valentine's Day—her favorite holiday—while she was surrounded by her family and her treasured collection of heart-shaped objects, her own heart stopped. She would have celebrated her 17th birthday the following month. After Amy's death, Mr. Lansworth arranged for Kory, her mother, and her grandfather to be flown out, and he honored them with a parade. Later there was an official ceremony to name the village's main street "Amy's Way."

Mrs. Johnson strongly believes that empathy is taught. "My daughter Kory developed empathy from having a terminally ill sister," she explains. "She saw the kinds of problems that our family, and other families, had to cope with. Just seeing other kids try to cope with being sick had an impact on her.

"I never prodded Kory to become an environmental activist, but she had seen me become deeply involved in pushing for some important reforms, so I am not surprised. It hasn't always been easy for her. Before middle school, the kids thought it was cool, but as they grew into young teens they would often tease her. One day some girls asked Kory if she liked a certain boy as a boyfriend, and she said no. They started to taunt her: 'Why not? 'Cause he doesn't recycle?' Middle-school kids can be cruel."

Kory continues to work with her family to fight what they call "environmental racism": situations in which the government or industry takes advantage of uninformed and usually poor communities. She encourages kids to learn about where they live and how to keep the land safe.

"Kory will take on issues that affect poor people," says Mrs. Johnson. "She is not shy. She gets up, tells our story, and tells people that they need to be involved and active in their communities. She has genuine empathy and truly cares for the handicapped, the homeless, and people with AIDS. She has respect for all these people."

Kory is very busy with school, but she still makes time for her volunteer work. She spends time at the local Ronald McDonald House, spending hours helping the staff clean and fix things up. (Like most teenagers, her own room is a mess.) She recently won $1,000 from Channel 12 in Arizona for the Twelve People Who Care Award; she gave $500 of her prize money to Body Positive, an Arizona AIDS project. This past summer, Kory and her mom helped raise money to rent a camp and give a summer vacation to 40 campers who have AIDS. Parents, doctors, psychologists, and educators volunteered in the effort. The camp was named Camp Hakuna Matata, after the song from *The Lion King*. It translates, roughly, to "no worries for the rest of our days."

Mrs. Johnson recalls: "One of the last camp activities for the campers, many of whom had been rejected by other programs, was a campfire. Each child threw a pinecone into the fire and said what they liked most about camp. Most of the children spoke about the acceptance and affection that they had found. Several children told us this was the first time people were not afraid to hug them."

When asked what parents can do to help raise compassionate children, Ms. Johnson replies, "Don't just tell your kids about the world and its problems. Show them. Don't always go to the mall on an outing. Take them to see a soup kitchen or a homeless shelter. Expose kids to things that are not too pretty. Don't just give your clothes to Goodwill. Take your children to meet the people who are getting the donations; they'll feel good if you do. And—I have to say this as someone who cares about the environment—don't just put out your bottles to be recycled. Take your kids to see what happens to those bottles. Show them what it means to recycle.

I took Kory with me to visit small towns to see the incinerators and to meet the people there. It makes much more of an impact on kids than reading about it in an article. As a parent, all I ever wanted was to raise children who care, who are respectful but who won't get walked on. I wanted them to know that they could make a difference. And I think they did."

AFTERWORD

It was an unusually warm March day in Billings, Montana, a day that was a harbinger of the early spring soon to descend upon the city. Three months after the dramatic events of the 1993 holiday season, I was visiting Billings to get a sense of the town, its people, and, most particularly, its children. Had youngsters been affected by what had occurred? If so, how?

I had been granted access to the Rimrock Elementary School, not far from the Schnitzers' home, and had been meeting with children from kindergarten through sixth grade, both individually and in groups.

An enticingly warm, soft breeze drifted through the classroom windows as we spoke. It was the sort of day when children strain to be outdoors and active. Yet there was no shortage of children who were willing and eager to talk with me. Christian or Jewish, white or black or Native American, they remembered the events vividly. One such group discussion, with third and fourth graders, was typical.

208

"It was the haters who did it," Charlene* stated loudly.

"They threw rocks at Isaac's menorah, just because he was Jewish," Daniel added.

"And they shouldn't do that," interrupted Matthew, "'cause it hurts people's feelings."

"If you don't stand up to bullies, they'll just keep pushing you around," Daniel offered.

"Yeah, so you have to do something," Jonathan stated flatly.

The children then went on to talk about the "Christmas menorahs" and how the town's actions had affected them. Every child I spoke with during these group interviews reported having had discussions with their parents about whether the family should display a menorah.

"I was scared," Max said. "We thought maybe we would have a rock thrown through *our* window. But my dad, he said it was the right thing to do. And my mom joked that we never liked our windows much, anyway."

"You just have to show people that you care," Jessica stated with conviction, summing up the past 40 minutes.

The children in Billings are, of course, well aware of the world's violence and injustice. But they are aware of something else as well: that their parents, teachers, and clergy are willing to reach out to help others in trouble, and to stand up to bullies and haters despite the risk of danger.

I found myself remembering Max's words durnig our group discussion. "I was scared," he had admitted. "But my dad, he said it was the right thing to do." Listening to Max and all the other children, I became convinced that

---

*The names of the Billings children have been changed.

they would remember that message because their families, neighbors, and *they themselves* had lived it.

With that kind of example, there is every reason to believe that these children's future actions will be influenced by what they learned, and that eventually they'll pass on their convictions to their own children and perhaps, to their children's children. When all is said and done, this may be Billings's greatest legacy.

As individuals, families, and communities, we too can pass on a similar legacy to our children by our words, our beliefs, and, most important, our actions. These actions needn't be as dramatic as those taken by the residents of Billings or by some of the other individuals profiled in this book. They can be quieter and simpler, but just as heartfelt, and just as crucial in shaping how children see themselves, others, and the world they live in.

Special Resources for Parents

Trying to raise compassionate, courageous children in a world filled with violence is not easy, as any parent knows. There are so many external forces that send negative messages to children *despite* adults' best efforts. Those forces will probably always be there, but the good news is that there are books, videos, and community programs that can aid parents' efforts by sending children the *right* kinds of messages. This appendix will identify and discuss some of the best resources available to parents, teachers, and other caring adults.

Tips from Specialized Programs

A number of specialized programs around the country promote caring and compassion in children in a variety of innovative ways. Among the best are the Giraffe Project, which encourages children to "stick their necks out" for the common good, Nursery Nature Walks, a program for children of all ages that encourages the development of empathy and tolerance in young children, and *The Puzzle Place*, a television program that promotes compassion and tolerance in young children. Each offers a number of intriguing activities that parents and teachers can use with children on an everyday basis.

The Giraffe Project

"People insist that there are no heroes anymore," says Ann Medlock, founder and president of the Giraffe Project. "Well, they're dead wrong. We find examples of our definition of a hero—someone who shows moral and intellectual courage despite risks or intimidation— on a regular basis. And the things these 'sung' and 'unsung' heroes have accomplished are pretty remarkable. It's our job to get the word out so children and adults can become aware that people like this (who are not so very different from the rest of us) do exist and are going strong."

Medlock had worked for many years as a publicist and freelance writer, but she became increasingly disturbed by the media's seeming determination to focus on what's wrong with our society instead of what's right. The last straw came when Medlock handed in an in-depth profile of a public figure to a newspaper editor.

His response was to ask for revisions. "'The story isn't

balanced. You have nothing negative about [this person.]'

"'But there *is* nothing negative,' she replied. 'I researched it; he's exactly as I've portrayed him—a dedicated, honest, and courageous man.'

"'Well, dig deeper and find something,' the editor insisted. 'Otherwise I can't use the piece.'

"I was livid," Medlock remembers, "because, yes, the world is a mess, but there are people who are doing some wonderful things and truly making a difference. What is it about the media—and our society—that makes us focus so much on the negative? Why is presenting the positive about people somehow suspect unless it's 'balanced' with the negative? There is something terribly wrong about this, I thought."

Thus was born the Giraffe Project. Its goal is to teach kids that goodness, courage, and heroism do exist, and that we can all strive for these qualities, no matter who we are. Supported largely by grants from private foundations, the program seeks to accomplish its goal this through training programs and through its curriculum for schools, Standing Tall.

Standing Tall finds contemporary, real-life heroes (Chapter Five: Exceptional Children . . . Exceptional Parents includes the stories of several of them) and works to publicize their deeds in local and national media. Unlike many existing character-education programs, says Medlock, in which students are presented with scenarios illustrating particular moral or ethical dilemmas and asked to discuss the "right" thing to do, Standing Tall does not try to lay down specific rules of conduct: "How can anyone teach character in a classroom in which some kids' parents support choice and others' folks picket abortion clinics? In which some kids have strong religious training and others none? In which some have been taught that homosexuality is immoral and others go home to gay parents? I believe that the Giraffe Project and its Standing Tall curriculum may have found a way that works, simply because we never thought of setting up debates on issues or presenting lists of values." Instead, Standing Tall highlights core principles that even people who disagree on issues can agree on. And it gets through what Medlock terms kids' "anti-message radar" by storytelling.

"If you think about it, it's clear that in every cultural tradition, people have taken ethical guidance from stories," says Medlock. "Humans love stories. They stick in our minds, even when we might brush off any principles embedded in them if they came at us as rules and admonitions."

After children participating in the curriculum learn about the heroes in these stories, they search for their own heroes—in the news, in books and movies, in their own communities and families. They then design a project for improving some aspect of the world around them. Medlock points out that the child's control over choosing this project is critical.

"Making their own observations and creating a response—rather than just signing up as troops in an existing service program—is critical to their sense of taking personal responsibility for something beyond their own lives. It also requires them to stretch; to get over their fears and their personal sense of limitation.

"We see kids starting out with great trepidation and

ending up with a sense of responsibility and self-respect that spills out all over their lives. The process has helped them come upon their own compassion and experience their connection to other individuals and to their community. They've found the courage to overcome their fears, they've seen that taking responsibility leads to results— and that the results are good.

"There's an underlying belief in all this that at the core, no matter how disconnected and uncaring they may have become, human beings are instinctively compassionate. That instinctive sense of connection is the place we must reach in each young human, getting past all that may be separating them from full involvement in the human family. They don't need to risk their lives to get there; they do need to absorb the stories of courageous, compassionate heroes. That's what the Giraffe Project is all about."

The Standing Tall program is being used in schools and in communities across the country. For information on how to establish the program in your community, call (360) 221–7989.

Programs such as the Giraffe Project and my own Heroes Project, which is being used in Newark, New Jersey, with mostly inner-city youngsters, attempt to help children examine and rethink their definition of what it means to be a hero. Instead of automatically equating heroes with celebrities or with physical strength and prowess, children in such programs look toward their families and communities to discover "unsung" heroes who have made a sacrifice, taken a risk to help others, or worked hard against the odds to achieve a personal dream. Most exciting, children are beginning to see how they can become their *own* heroes by showing those old-fashioned attributes that are starting to come back into style—courage, caring, and fortitude.

Parents, teachers, and other adults can encourage children to look in the right places for genuine hero material. Following are some suggestions for getting started.

- Talk with children about what it means to be a hero. Let them know what your definition of heroism is.
- Begin an ongoing dialogue with children about who their heroes are. (You might be surprised.) Ask them why they made their choices.
- Look within your family to find examples of unsung heroes. Who did something that made a change for the better in the family or the community? Who stood up for a personal belief in the face of unpopularity, ridicule, or hostility? Who made a personal sacrifice for the sake of others? Who worked hard to achieve a personal dream against many odds? Who inspired others to do "good deeds" or to follow their dreams? Often parents neglect to tell their children these stories, perhaps feeling that a tale of a relative's courage that occurred 20 or 30 or 60 years ago is simply not relevant to young people's lives today. But these family stories can have a profound impact on youngsters, including anchoring them to family traditions and values. Would the adolescent who scrawled anti- Semitic graffiti on the synagogue in Clifton, New Jersey, have done so if he had known

that his grandfather had risked his life during the Holocaust to save a Jewish neighbor? His parents will never know.

- Ask children if they feel that they could ever be a hero. Discuss with them the reasons for their answers.
- Let children know that you feel they do have the capacity for compassion, courage, and initiative. Point out to them the things they may already be doing that are heroic; for example, coping with a disability, working hard toward a dream, resisting the temptation to smoke cigarettes or try drugs, "being there" for a friend or family member, or sticking up for a belief.
- Remember that children learn heroic traits by example, and their most important examples are their parents, along with relatives, teachers, and other models in the community.

For further information about The Heroes Project, call (201) 926–2648.

Nursery Nature Walks

For many years, naturalists have understood that nature walks could greatly enhance children's appreciation of the natural environment. Now educators, mental-health professionals, and parents are beginning to understand that certain kinds of nature walks can enhance children's appreciation of the *human* environment as well.

Nursery Nature Walks, a unique program in greater Los Angeles, helps children of *all* ages to understand and be sensitive to diversity in nature and the right of all living things to be treated with consideration and respect. The program consists of a series of two-hour group walks with children, parents, and teachers, led by specially trained leaders called docents.

Andrea Diamond, the program's docent in charge of developing activities for selected Los Angeles schools, described the program's purpose in a recent interview: "Interestingly, the parents and teachers who accompany children on these walks are just as enthusiastic as the children, finding that they learn a number of lessons of their own. To begin to enhance adult awareness of what nature can teach children, we might ask parents and teachers something like, 'When was the last time you gave the right of way to a stick bug crossing your path instead of instinctively stepping on it?'

"Most adults, we've found, tend not to consciously think of these things. And so children miss opportunities for some important life lessons. Participating in these walks with their children gives parents and teachers a number of specific teaching tools, while their kids experience a lot of fun. They don't feel like they are learning a lesson, and perhaps that's the key to our success. For example, we try to educate children about the importance of people working together by studying something like an ant hill. It's informative and enjoyable for kids, and much more effective than a typical lecture they might get from an adult about the importance of cooperation.

"Another example might be to show children how a

destructive act of nature—like a forest fire—has an impact on many living things, like the trees, insects, plant life, birds, flowers, and everything else. We show how everything in our environment is interconnected and what one destructive act can do. Then we relate this to the children's own neighborhoods. We start with the elemental, then build up to more complex concepts involving how we should treat one another and be treated ourselves.

"Many of our children from inner-city Los Angeles have never been to the beach or to any other kind of natural environment. It's quite an experience for them in terms of getting a sense of nature and the interconnectedness of living things. They begin to understand what it means to harm trees and grass, and how that affects different birds and insects. We then try to relate this theme to an urban environment. Very often this is a totally new idea to children.

"We don't pick flowers or other plants. That's never allowed, though the children, of course, want to. We emphasize that if everyone picked the flowers there would be no flowers left for others to enjoy, and that the bees need flowers to make honey. It's a simple concept, but it goes so deep. It means learning to think about others. It's kind of like preparing children to go to a museum and view a painting without trying to take it off the wall and take it home. We try to translate that concept into children's interactions with others, emphasizing that no one can own or control another person.

"We also teach the importance of preserving the natural environment for ourselves and others. We want to make children think about the consequences of paving over the grass and lands. Building things is not always progress. A lot of children in L.A. constantly observe buildings being knocked down and grass being covered over with concrete. Kids love tractors, big machines, and loud noises. So they enjoy these kinds of scenes. But digging up the earth and cutting down trees are done at a cost. It's important that children understand this. Often it's something that they've never thought about.

"There was one occasion when I was with a group of children and we came upon a poison-oak plant. I explained that it was dangerous, that they had to stay away from it. A couple of the kids ran and got a stick and came back and started to hit it; kind of a learned reaction that when something might hurt you, you have to resort to violence to protect yourself. We teach children that if something is dangerous in nature, it's sometimes best to avoid it; that violence or striking out does not have to be the answer. For example, when a wasp lands on a child's hat because the hat's a pretty yellow color, we stress that the best way that child can protect him or herself from getting stung is not to try to kill that wasp but to be able to show patience and stand still until the wasp flies away. That's what will keep the child safe. We try to consistently reinforce these kinds of reactions as an alternative to violence or hitting.

"I remember one incident, at the beginning of this past summer, shortly after there had been reports of mountain-lion attacks in the news. When some of the parents brought up their concern about the lions, some of the kids said that if they saw a mountain lion, they would kill him right away. The walk leader pointed out that people present a bigger threat to animals because we don't need a reason like survival to kill; that most animals don't kill or attack except when they're hunting for food or to protect themselves and their young. They had no idea. Violence, to them, just seemed to go along with being big and powerful."

For information about starting a Nursery Nature Walk program in your own community, call (310) 998–1151.

For those who don't have such a program nearby, Andrea Diamond suggests that parents try the following activities with their children.

Ant Farm: By observing an ant farm, a child can gain a new appreciation of these insects, their special duties, and how they work so well together as a community. While observing these creatures' movements, ask your children such questions as: "Can you think of any other examples of someone or something being small but very strong and mighty, like an ant?" "Can you think of some reasons why working as a team in a community, such as ants do in their ant farm, can be important?"

Butterflies Are Free: Many pet stores carry caterpillars ready to spin their cocoons in small "cocoon houses." Your child can watch with wonder the transformation of a cocoon to a beautiful butterfly, then free the butterfly outside. Talk with your child about how wonderful it is to admire something beautiful and then give it back to nature. It isn't necessary to own things of beauty in order to get enjoyment from them. When taking a walk or passing a bed of beautiful flowers or interesting rocks, talk to your child about how beautiful nature is and how nice it is to leave beauty where we found it so the whole neighborhood can enjoy it.

Many Colors: This activity is especially fun in the autumn. Ask your child to color a picture of some trees. Give her many colors, excluding green, then see what she comes up with. Talk to her about the many colors that make up a tree. Alternatively, take fallen leaves and crumble them into small pieces. Your child can put glue on construction paper, then sprinkle the crumbled leaves on the glue and tap off the excess. Discuss with your child the beauty and importance of diversity in the colors of nature. Tell your child that many colors make up a picture. Point out that the world is full of people of many colors, and that this makes the world more interesting and beautiful. This dialogue builds an appreciation for diversity in people by observing nature.

Crystal Colors: Hang a crystal in the kitchen window or on the rearview mirror of your car. Have your child try to catch the rainbows that the prism makes in his hands. Ask him: "Do you know why rainbows are thought to be the most beautiful sight in nature?" The answer: Because a rainbow has every color in it, just as our planet has people of all colors.

Culture Kitchen: Grow an herb garden to teach your child about caring for something and watching it grow. Then show her how to reap what she harvested in the family kitchen. Make a soup or stew from an ethnic recipe. Talk to your child about ethnic foods, and how lucky we are to have so many cultures in our neighborhood, city, and country to enjoy.

Web of Beauty: Find a spiderweb and show your child how to mist the web lightly with water to make it visible. Talk to your child about how smart the spider must be to make such an intricate, beautiful web. Point out how delicate the web is, and that it's important for us to respect spiders' webs, which they use to catch their food. Have your child paint a web with white glue onto black or blue construction paper. Pour on glitter and tap off the excess. Make a spider out of a black pipe cleaner. Now play "Interview with a Spider," in which your child plays the spider. Ask him: "Why did you make this web?" "Was it difficult?" "How long did it take?" "How would you feel if someone threw a ball through it and destroyed it?" "Would you make another one, and would you make it in the same place or move to another place?" This discussion builds empathy for small creatures' homes.

Bird Watch: Attracting birds by feeding them is a good lesson for children. Take a pinecone and cover it with peanut butter. Hang it by a string in a place where your child can watch the activity. Then talk to your child about the habits of birds. (The local library can help with information.) Discuss birds' nesting habits, such as building soft nests in safe places (e.g., inside a rosebush that has protective thorns). Point out that birds take good care of their babies when they are born. This dialogue helps children understand what caring and nurturing mean. If you can, find a real bird's nest that's been used and abandoned in order to show your child up close the intricate handiwork that a bird uses to make a nest.

The Puzzle Place

Several years ago, the Corporation for Public Broadcasting (CPB) asked for proposals to create a unique children's program that would help preschoolers, ages two to five, understand the need to treat others with tolerance, compassion, and respect. In a world where even very young children see so many examples of people treating others with insensitivity and disrespect, the need for such a program seemed compelling, even urgent. But how could it be done in a way that was entertaining and engaging rather than preachy?

Suzanne Singer, a producer for Los Angeles's public TV station KCET, teamed with Cecily Truett and Larry Lancit, principals of Lancit Media Productions in New York, and developed the concept for *The Puzzle Place*, a half-hour daily television show for children and their parents or caretakers to watch together.

"*The Puzzle Place* is actually a place children get to through their imaginations," Singer explains. "It is a safe environment where children can be introduced to, and try out, new concepts. There are no adults in *The Puzzle Place*; it is a place where kids learn to work things out for themselves."

The Puzzle Place features six "puppet kids" with distinct personalities. They come from different parts of the country and have diverse racial and cultural backgrounds. Each puppet is unique; none of them is meant to represent an entire race, culture, or religion. The puppets show how people who are different can get along and appreciate the many things they share in common.

Using these characters, *The Puzzle Place* aims to foster the kinds of moral and social traits that are so crucial to children today. These include empathy and compassion, tolerance, self-esteem, and an ability to identify and solve the problems that youngsters will inevitably confront in this society.

"The goals we set for this program were very challenging—sometimes even daunting," says Singer. "For example, how could we effectively teach youngsters about the importance of accepting and appreciating diversity when preschoolers don't know what a culture or a country is. We are trying to focus on a concept which they usually can't quite grasp yet. So what we do is try to establish building blocks that will eventually lead to this kind of understanding, one block at a time, one episode at a time. For the most part, children of this age tend to be quite self-centered, so teaching them about tolerance and empathy can be tricky. Certainly preschoolers can respond to others who are hurting or upset. But this show tries to go beyond that and aims to teach children to put themselves in another person's shoes.

"In *The Puzzle Place*, the puppets really listen to each other. They put their arms around each other and talk through problems that come up. They don't reprimand each other or deny their feelings; they gently try to explain how they feel and try to give help and support to one another. In each episode, we make an attempt to specifically model how kids can be empathic, caring people and good friends, as well as effective problem-solvers. We do this in a way that we believe entertains and engages.

"The concepts of problem-solving, taking action, and working cooperatively are key issues that are addressed in episode after episode. The reality is, these kids will be growing up in an increasingly diverse and complex world. We want them to be sensitive and kind toward others, but we also want them to learn to work cooperatively to identify problems and make choices about how to deal with those problems. We believe *The Puzzle Place* helps kids to accomplish this."

How can parents and other caring adults maximize the impact of *The Puzzle Place* and shows like it? The show's creative staff and professional advisers offer these suggestions for increasing children's sensitivity to the diversity around them:

- Look for pictures that can expand a child's vision of the world. Choose images that counter the influence of negative pictures your children are likely to see when they are not in your care. Avoid pictures that repeat stereotypes, such as a picture in an alphabet book of a warrior in headdress under "I is for Indian."
- Include many different options for skin colors in your crayon and paint boxes, clay, and construction paper.
- Provide dolls of varying ethnicities, races, shapes, sizes, and physical abilities.
- Broaden children's vision by providing as many different kinds of materials as possible. Different environments can include farm, city, waterfront, jungle, desert, and forest; choose different kinds of hats for different professions and animals from different parts of the world. Provide toys that encourage rather than limit imagination, such as

generic dolls instead of characters from a prime-time TV show.

- If you have a play kitchen, gather cooking and eating utensils of different ethnicities (for example, chopsticks and a wok in addition to forks and a pan).
- Put up a mirror so that children can see what they look like and get a sense of how they are both unique and like others.
- Pay attention to your use of the word "we": "I won't see you next week because we are all going to take some time off to celebrate Christmas with our families." Do you really mean everyone?
- Use nonsexist terms such as "firefighter" instead of "fireman," or "mail carrier" instead of "mailman." If the books you are reading aloud use terms that exclude, change them.

Children's experience of the world is limited; they tend to accept as true much of what they see on television. For that reason, it is important to pay attention to what they are viewing, and to provide real-life experiences that counter the negative stereotypes presented on TV.

For further information about The Puzzle Place, *call your local PBS station or Simone Bloom. at (617) 566–0093.*

USING STORIES TO TEACH COMPASSION AND COURAGE

Stories, whether true or fictional, have the potential to

delight, inspire, and motivate children. But their effectiveness in teaching life's lessons depends not just on their content but on how they are used.

Storytelling Tips

Following are some guidelines for maximizing a story's meaning or lesson. These apply whether the story is read, told, or seen.

- Help children relate these stories to their own lives, families, and communities.
- Discuss the characters' choices with children. Did they agree with the choices? Why? What choices would they have made?
- Help children think of different solutions and endings for the stories. This helps develop their imagination and problem-solving skills.
- Take your cues from your children regarding what part of the story they find most interesting. Then try to focus on that.

Let's look at how parents and other adults might discuss a story with their children, using my book *The Christmas Menorahs: How a Town Fought Hate* (Albert Whitman, 1995). After reading the story, parents and teachers can ask children to think about these questions:

1. Why do you think people sometimes hate other people just because of their skin color or their reli-

gion or because of where they come from?

2. Is it ever okay to hate people for that reason? Why?
3. Are there haters in our community?
4. Who are they?
5. Who are the people that they hate?
6. Why do they hate them?
7. Do you think what happened in Billings could happen in our town?
8. What do you think our family and neighbors would do?
9. What would *you* do?
10. What do you think about what Issac and Teresa did? Do you agree with their actions?
11. How can we be a good friend to people who are the target of haters?
12. Why is it good for us to stand up to haters?

Recommended Books That Teach Compassion and Courage

The following is a list of recommended titles* for parents, teachers, and other adults to share with the children in their care. Some of the recommendations include suggested questions to get your children thinking about the issues raised by the stories. Grade levels indicate approximate reading levels

---

*This list was prepared with the assistance of Mary Riskind, manager of youth services at the Montclair, New Jersey, Public Library, and Maggie Shoemaker, manager of children's services at the Englewood, New Jersey, Public Library.

for independent reading and are intended as guides only. Many communities offer interlibrary loan service if a book you need is not available at your neighborhood library.

Ben and the Porcupine, by Carol Carrick (preschool–grade 2). Christopher's dog Ben comes home one evening with a painful mustache of porcupine quills. Christopher is worried that his dog will be hurt again, so he devises a special solution to keep his pet out of harm's way. Christopher's answer to his problem requires the sacrifice of a prized personal possession. Caring for others sometimes requires that the caregiver give up something valuable—whether it's time, talents, or personal belongings—in exchange for another's well-being. Can you think of instances in which someone, perhaps a family member or a friend, took care of you at some personal cost? Are there instances in which you have shared what you had in order to show that you cared for another?

Animal stories often demonstrate issues of compassion and call upon a child's ingenuity to solve problems. Look, for instance, at *Thy Friend, Obadiah*, by Brinton Turkle, a picture story of a Quaker child who makes friends with a pesky seagull. Older readers will enjoy *The Trouble with Tuck*, by Theodore Taylor, in which a young girl struggles with how to care for her blind dog. *Shiloh*, a morally complex novel by Phyllis Reynolds Naylor, pits the welfare of an abused dog against a boy's understanding that outright theft is wrong. For each story, have children consider how else they might have solved the dilemma of caring for these animals.

Number the Stars, by Lois Lowry (grades 4–6). Set during

World War II, this Newbery Award–winning book tells the story of Danish resistance to Nazi occupation from the point of view of 10-year-old Annemarie Johansen. Annemarie exhibits courage and intelligence as she helps to smuggle her best friend's parents to Sweden while her friend Ellen Rosen stays on, posing as another child in the Johansen family. Based on a historical incident, this novel is remarkable for the credible heroism of its young protagonist and makes a good first book about the Holocaust for young readers.

Adults and children will want to ask themselves how they would have responded to the peril of the Rosen family. Most of us are seldom confronted with life-or-death situations that threaten friends and neighbors. My book *The Christmas Menorahs: How a Town Fought Hate* is a modern-day example of a less extreme situation that nonetheless jeopardizes the rights and safety of members of a community. Can you think of past events in your own town or neighborhood that might have called for similar acts of concern?

Other fictionalized accounts of World War II heroism and children are told in Marie McSwigan's *Snow Treasure*, the story of Norwegian children who transport the village's silver on daily sled runs to a secure hiding place in full view of Nazi soldiers, and in Claire Bishop's *Twenty and Ten*, a story of French children who hide Jewish orphans.

Pink and Say, by Patricia Polacco (grades 1–3). A story handed down from Civil War times to the present by the author's family, this moving picture book is the account of the friendship forged between two teenage boys, both

Union soldiers, one white, one African-American. Pinkus Aylee, or Pink, finds a mortally wounded white boy left for dead on the battlefield; without Pink's help, the boy is sure to die. Pink and his slave mother, Moe Moe, nurse the young soldier, who confesses to being a deserter, back to both spiritual and physical health. In the end, Pink and his mother pay with their lives at the hands of Confederates, leaving only 15-year-old Sheldon Russell Curtis, author Polacco's great-great grandfather, to remember and to honor their bravery.

Family stories can be important in helping to establish for younger members what is valued in the family. Does your family have favorite stories that are a tradition?

The history of racism in our country offers many opportunities to discuss the personal price paid by our forebears for freedom. Written for older elementary readers, *Roll of Thunder, Hear My Cry*, a Depression-era story by Mildred Taylor, and *Words by Heart*, by Ouida Sebestyen, are the accounts of African-American families who hold firm to their self-respect despite the threats and indignities heaped on them by their neighbors. In Patricia Beatty's *Lupita Mañana*, a determined young Mexican girl immigrates illegally to the United States to help support her impoverished family. Younger readers will respond to Ken Mochizuki's picture book *Baseball Saved Us*, about life in a Japanese internment camp, and to *Teammates*, by Peter Golenbeck, the story of Jackie Robinson, the first African-American to play major-league baseball.

Poppy, by Avi (grades 4–6). The great horned owl Mr. Ocax controls Dimwood Forest and the tiny deer mice by pretending to be their protector. Poppy's disobedience puts the entire mouse community at risk. As she attempts to face up to the trouble she has caused, Poppy discovers what a terrible lie has been foisted on them all and in the end confronts Mr. Ocax.

This animal fable is a story of both the power of truth and the importance of self-determination. Before you and your child read this story together you might think about this saying: "The truth shall set you free." How does learning the truth set Poppy free? Can you think of some historical examples of persons or groups who were controlled, perhaps enslaved, because they were deprived of information or knowledge? Read *The Giver*, by Lois Lowry, and compare the circumstances of the young hero of this novel with those of Poppy and her deer-mice family.

Avi is a versatile writer who often addresses questions of conscience. Look for other titles by this author, such as *Night Journeys*, set in the Colonial era, and *Nothing But the Truth*, a young adult novel that raises questions about the nature of patriotism and freedom of speech.

Uncle Willie and the Soup Kitchen, by DyAnne DiSalvo-Ryan (preschool–grade 2). A young boy is curious and maybe a little embarrassed that his Uncle Willie works in the soup kitchen. He goes to help out at the kitchen one day and gets to know the Can Man and the homeless woman who sleeps on the bench. Best of all, he has a good time.

DiSalvo-Ryan's story is a nonthreatening introduction to the problems of poverty for younger readers. Be prepared to address questions of how people become hungry and homeless. Ask children to think about how someone might fall into those circumstances. This story is also an effective demonstration that even the very young can help their less fortunate neighbors. Ask the children in your care to think of someone they know who might need their help. How can they be of service?

For other sensitive treatments of contemporary social problems, turn to books by the prolific Eve Bunting, such as *Fly Away Home*, the story of a homeless boy living at the airport with his father, or *The Wednesday Surprise*, the story of a young schoolgirl who teaches her grandmother to read. Alzheimer's is the focus of *The Memory Box*, by Mary Bahr. For a lighter, equally caring treatment of aging, look at Mem Fox's books *Wilfred Gordon McDonald Partridge* and *Night Noises*.

More too-good-to-miss books include:

Wagon Wheels, by Barbara Brenner (beginning reader). Based on historical fact, this is the story of black pioneers who went West after the Civil War in search of free land. Three boys wait in a Kansas dugout, then travel 150 miles to find their father and the new home he has built for them. With the help of the Osage Indians, they survive hunger, prairie fire, and wild animals. For similar tales of pioneer courage, see *The Courage of Sarah Noble*, by Alice Dalgliesh, and *The Sign of the Beaver*, by Elizabeth George Speare.
Summer Wheels, by Eve Bunting (grades 2–3). The Bicyle Man lends bicycles to children in the neighborhood for free as long as they observe two simple rules: Return the bicycle by four o'clock and, if it breaks while you have it, fix it. A new boy shows up who does not seem to understand the rules. Lawrence and Brady learn what the Bicycle Man already knows: that sometimes "attitude" is

a mask for the troubled person beneath.

Cracker Jackson, by Betsy Byars (grades 4–6). Cracker Jackson is certain that his former baby-sitter, now friend, is being abused by her husband. Jackson is determined to save Alma and her baby, no matter what the danger to himself. This is a warm, funny story told by a master storyteller. One note of caution: Cracker Jackson sets off on a wild drive in a car he can barely handle. Young readers will not miss the lesson—that this is an example not to be followed—but it deserves reinforcement by adults.

No Good in Art, by Miriam Cohen (preschool–grade 1). The appreciation and encouragement of Jim's classmates help him understand that his artwork is beautiful, too. Cohen's first-grade stories handle the ordinary yet serious problems of children with humor and empathy. Look for other titles in this series: *Will I Have a Friend?*, *Best Friends*, *When Will I Read?*, and *It's George!*

The Whipping Boy, by Sid Fleischmann (grades 3–4). Told with a dollop of humor, this is the story of Prince Brat and Jemmy-of-the-Streets, who is forced by custom to take the badly behaved prince's thrashings. In a twist of fate, the two boys are captured by outlaws. In order to survive, they swap roles, and Prince Brat finally learns how to take his own punishment.

Stone Fox, John Reynolds Gardiner (grades 2–4). Willy is determined to save his sick grandfather's farm. He harvests the potato crop himself. Now he has to come up with money to pay off back taxes. He pins his hopes on winning a national dogsled race, but he has to compete against Stone Fox, a Shoshone Indian who has always won the race, and whose dream is to return his people to their land.

Set aside a box of tissue for the dramatic conclusion.

Amazing Grace, by Mary Hoffman (preschool–grade 2). When her class decides to present the play *Peter Pan*, Grace auditions for the part of Peter despite the reservations of her classmates about a girl—and a black girl, at that—playing the role. Grace's imagination and the support of her loving family give her the strength to prove that she can be whatever she wants to be. Courage comes in many forms, including the determination to be who you truly are.

A Night Without Stars, by James Howe (grades 5–6). Maria needs open-heart surgery. Frightened by what is ahead for her, she seeks solace from a fellow patient the other kids call the Monster Man, a badly disfigured burn patient. Having survived several operations, Donald helps Maria to cope with her fears, and Maria in turn helps Donald to heal the scars left by years of mistrust and loneliness.

Hang Tough, Paul Mather, by Alfred Slote (grades 4–5). Slote's baseball stories are often stories of fighting the odds and finding the courage from within to persevere. Paul Mather loves baseball; moreover, his team needs his pitching arm. It seems particularly cruel when Paul is diagnosed with leukemia in the middle of the season and has to give up baseball to undergo treatment. But Paul is a winner, even from the confines of his wheelchair.

Somebody Loves You, Mr. Hatch, by Eileen Spinelli (preschool–grade 2). Even Mr. Hatch describes himself as a man who keeps to himself. One day, by accident, the postman delivers a surprise package that contains the note "Somebody loves you." Mr. Hatch's behavior changes, until he discovers the package was a mistake. Mr. Hatch's newfound friends notice the difference and respond as real friends do. It takes just one to be lonely, more to make friends.

Save Halloween, by Stephanie Tolan (grades 4–6). When Johanna volunteers to write the class Halloween play, she doesn't anticipate the conflict that occurs between her project and her family's fundamentalist Christian beliefs. This is a thought-provoking story for children, exploring issues of religious belief, independence, and commitment.

A Dog Called Kitty, by Bill Wallace (grades 4–5). Overcoming personal fears can require both stamina and courage. Traumatized as a young child by a dog bite, the narrator lives with the embarrassment that his phobia causes him among family and friends until he finally decides to confront his enemy. See also *Call It Courage*, written by Armstrong Sperry and set in the Polynesian Islands, in which a boy conquers his fear of the sea.

Kate Shelley and the Midnight Express, by Margaret K. Wetterer (beginning reader). This is the true story of a 15-year-old Iowa girl who braves a heavy storm, crossing a washed-out railroad bridge on her hands and knees, in order to stop the express train that's due at midnight. Kate's reward for saving so many lives that night was a lifetime railroad pass and a personal stop whenever she wanted—right in front of her house.

The list of books only begins here. Fine instructive and inspirational stories abound. Consult your children's librarian for assistance in selecting additional titles.

Recommended Videos That Teach Compassion and Courage

These videos* are generally appropriate for children in grades three and up, but this will vary depending upon the child. Parents and teachers may want to preview the videos to determine suitability before sharing them with children.

And the Children Shall Lead (WonderWorks). When a group of civil rights activists come to Catesville, Mississippi, in 1964, 12-year-old Rachel and her friends persuade the adults to overcome the racial barriers that divide them.

Bridge of Adam Rush (Time-Life). Set in the rural America of a century ago, this is the story of 12-year-old Adam's struggle to complete the construction of an all-important bridge after his stepfather is injured in an accident.

Caddie Woodlawn (WonderWorks). A spirited 11-year-old growing up in the wilds of 1860s Wisconsin, Caddie plays a key role in keeping the peace between the settlers and the Dakota Indians.

Charlotte's Web (Paramount). This animated story is based on the wonderful book by E.B. White about a girl, a little pig, and a wise spider named Charlotte. The story focuses on friendship, acceptance, and coming to terms with the inevitable losses that life brings.

The Chronicles of Narnia (WonderWorks). This series consists of three video sets: *The Lion, the Witch and the Wardrobe, Prince Caspian and the Voyage of the Dawn Treader*, and *The Silver Chair*. Based upon the books by

*This list was prepared with the assistance of John Skillin, audiovisual librarian at the Montclair, New Jersey, Public Library.

C.S. Lewis, these imaginative stories take place in a beguiling magical kingdom. At one level an allegory for the battle between good and evil, the stories touch upon the themes of faith, loyalty, betrayal, courage, and forgiveness.

Daniel and the Towers (WonderWorks). In 1954, 10-year-old Daniel Guerra is befriended by the eccentric sculptor Simon Rodia and leads the fight to save Rodia's life's work from being demolished.

Follow the North Star (Time-Life). In this suspenseful story of the underground railroad, a young white Northerner risks his life by traveling to Maryland in order to rescue a slave and bring him North to freedom.

The Four Diamonds (Walt Disney). A moving story about a young adolescent's battle with cancer and the courage, creativity, and strength of will he uses to cope with the disease. As his illness affects his family and friends, they try to understand and respond to his emotional needs. This video is most appropriate for preadolescents and adolescents.

Hoosiers (Orion). This is a personal favorite of mine. Based on the true story of a small-town Indiana Basketball team, this tale explores issues of compassion, redemption, personal courage, and what it means to be part of a team. Entertaining as well as inspiring, this film is greatly enjoyed by both children and adults.

Island of the Blue Dolphins (Universal). When a native girl's family flees its island home, leaving the girl's brother behind, she jumps ship and remains on the island for the next 20 years. This tale of survival is based on a true story.

Journey of Natty Gann (Walt Disney). During the Great Depression, a teenage girl travels cross-country alone in search of her father.

King of the Hill (Gramercy). A self-reliant boy of 12, Aaron is left alone and hungry when his mother is hospitalized and his father is forced to leave town in pursuit of a job. Even so, he manages to triumph over many obstacles to finish the school year with honors.

Rookie of the Year (20th Century-Fox). In this charming fantasy, 12-year-old Henry leads the last-place Chicago Cubs to World Series glory.

Walkabout (20th Century-Fox). Two children lost in the Australian outback are led to safety by a young aborigine. This award-winning film is notable for its outstanding cinematography.

A Waltz Through the Hills (WonderWorks). A recently orphaned brother and sister fear they will be placed in foster homes. To prevent this, they set off on a hazardous journey across the wilderness in the hope of reaching a ship that will take them to England and their only surviving relatives.

NOTES

INTRODUCTION

1. D. Prothrow-Stith, *Deadly Consequences: How Violence Is Destroying Our Teenage Population and a Plan to Begin Solving the Problem* (New York: Harper Collins, 1991).

2. 1993 FBI statistics.

3. R. Dunlap, A. Beigel, and V. Armon, "Young Children and the Watts Revolt," *Community Mental Health Journal* 4 (1968): 201–10.

   H. Landgarten, M. Junge, M. Tasem, and M. Walson, "Art Therapy as a Modality for Crisis Intervention: Children Express Reactions to Violence in Their Community," *Clinical Social*

Work Journal 6 (1978): 221–29.

J. Nemtzow and S. R. Lesser, "Reactions of Parents and Children to the Death of President Kennedy," *Journal of Orthopsychiatry* 34 (1964): 280–81.

R. E. Schwartz, "Children under Fire: The Role of the Schools," *American Journal of Orthopsychiatry* 52 (1982): 409–19.

CHAPTER 1

1. Survey conducted by the Times Mirror Center for the People and the Press as reported in "Survey Finds Voters in U.S. Rootless and Self-Absorbed," *The New York Times,* 21 September 1994.

   Survey conducted by Independent Sector as reported in "Less Money and Time for Charity, Study Says," *The New York Times,* 20 October 1994.

2. For example, the 1989 study conducted by Dr. Myra Weissman, New York State Psychiatric Institute/Columbia Presbyterian Medical Center, as reported in "A Rising Cost of Modernity: Depression," *The New York Times,* 8 December 1992.

3. A. Campell, *The Sense of Well-Being in America: Recent Patterns and Trends* (New York: McGraw Hill, 1980).

J. L. Freedman, *Happy People: What Happiness Is, Who Has It, and Why* (New York: Harcourt Brace Jovanovich, 1978).

G. Sheehy, *Pathfinders* (New York: William Morrow, 1981).

4. January 1996 telephone interview with Dr. Diane Tice to discuss research she conducted at Case Western Reserve University from 1990 to 1993.

   July 1995 telephone interview with Dr. Nancy Eisenberg, University of Arizona, regarding ongoing research she has conducted and her knowledge of the literature.

   July 1995, August 1995, and October 1995 telephone interviews with Dr. Ervin Staub, University of Massachusetts, regarding ongoing research he has conducted and his knowledge of the literature.

5. T. Achenbach and C. T. Howell, "Are American Children's Problems Getting Worse? A 13-Year Comparison," *Journal of the American Academy of Child and Adolescent Psychiatry* 32 (1993): 1145–54.

   A. Angold and E. J. Costello, "Depressive Comorbidity in Children and Adolescents: Empirical, Theoretical and Methodological Issues," *American Journal of Psychiatry* 150 (1993): 1779–91.

6. Telephone interview with Dr. Diane Tice to discuss research she conducted at Case Western Reserve from 1990 to 1993. Dr. Tice was the lead investigator.

7. Telephone interview with Dr. Staub, July 1995.

8. M. Barnett, et al., "Empathy in Young Children: Relation to Parents' Empathy, Affection, and Emphasis on the Feelings of Others," *Developmental Psychology* 16 (1980): 243–44.

   N. Eisenberg-Berg and P. Mussen, "Empathy and Moral Development in Adolescence," *Developmental Psychology* 14 (1978): 185–86.
   M. L. Hoffman, "Development of Prosocial Motivation: Empathy and Guilt," in *The Development of Prosocial Behavior*, ed. N. Eisenberg (New York: Academic Press, 1982).

9. Telephone interview with Dr. Mark Barnett, June 1995.

10. Telephone interview with Dr. Staub, July 1995.

11. Interview "Studies on Development of Empathy Challenge Some Old Assumptions," *The New York Times,* 12 July 1990.

12. Telephone interview with Dr. Staub, July 1995.

13. Telephone interview with Dr. Earl Schaeffer, lead inves-

tigator of the University of North Carolina study.

14. D. Baumrind, "Current Patterns of Parental Authority," Developmental Psychology Monographs, no. 4: 1–103.

N. Eisenberg, et al. "The Relation of Empathy Related Emotions and Maternal Practices to Children's Comforting Behavior," *Journal of Experimental Child Psychology* 55 (1993): 130–50.

M. L. Hoffman, "Moral Internalization, Parental Power, and the Nature of Parent-Child Interaction," *Developmental Psychology* 11 (1975): 228–37.

15. C. Zahn-Wexler, M. Radke-Yarrow, and R. A. King, "Child Rearing and Children's Prosocial Initiations Towards Victims of Distress," *Child Development* 50 (1979): 319–30.

16. S. P. Oliner and P. M. Oliner, *The Altruistic Personality: Rescuers of Jews in Nazi Europe* (New York: Free Press, 1988).

17. Interview and background information about Dr. Rosenhan's work "Why Do Some People Turn Away from Others in Trouble?" *The New York Times,* 13 July 1981.

18. Ibid.

19. Telephone interview with Dr. Rosenhan, October 1995.

20. Interview "Why Do Some People Turn Away from Others in Trouble?" *The New York Times,* 13 July 1981.

21. Telephone interview with Dr. Staub, July 1995.

22. Ibid.

23. T. Keneally, *Schindler's List* (New York: Simon & Schuster, 1982).

24. S. P. Oliner and P. M. Oliner, *The Altruistic Personality: Rescuers of Jews in Nazi Europe* (New York: Free Press, 1988) 134–35.

25. Telephone interview with Dr. Staub, July 1995.

26. Telephone interview with Dr. Eisenberg, July 1995.

27. Telephone interview with Dr. Grollman, June 1995.

29. M. A. Barnett, "Empathy and Related Responses in Children," in *Empathy and its Development*, eds. N. Eisenberg and J. Strayer (New York: Cambridge University Press, 1987) 146–62.

30. Ibid.

31. Telephone interview with Dr. Grollman, June 1995.

32. J. E. Gruseo, "Socializing Concern for Others in the Home," *Developmental Psychology* 27 (1991): 338–42.

33. Telephone interview with Dr. Staub, July 1995.

34. Telephone interview with Dr. Grollman, June 1995.

35. A. Mehrabian and N. Epstein, "A Measure of Emotional Empathy," *Journal of Personality* 40 (1972): 525–43.

36. N. D. Feshback, "Sex Differences in Empathy and Social Behavior in Children," in *The Development of Prosocial Behavior*, ed. N. Eisenberg (New York: Academic Press, 1982).

37. R. Koestner, C. Franz, and J. Weinberger, "The Family Origins of Empathic Concern: A 26-Year Longitudinal Study," *Journal of Personality and Social Psychology* 58 (1990): 709–17.

38. Interview "Studies on Development of Empathy Challenge. Same Old Assumptions." *The New York Times,* 12 July 1990.

39. Telephone interview with Dr. Eisenberg, July 1995.

40. Ibid.

41. "Studying the Pivotal Role of Bystanders," *The New York Times,* 22 June 1993.

42. Telephone interview with Dr. Staub, July 1995.

43. Ibid.

44. Ibid.

45. Interview with Mr. Lerman "Spreading History's Truth About the Holocaust," *The New York Times,* 11 September 1994.

CHAPTER 2

1. Interview "TV: Getting a Close Look as a Contributor to Real Violence," *The New York Times,* 14 December 1994.

2. For example:
   A. C. Nielson Company, Nielson Report on Television (Northbrook, Ill.: Nielson Media Research, 1990).

3. G. Gerbner, et al., "The Demonstration of Power: Violence Profile No. 10," in 1978 report issued by Cultural Indicators Research Team, Annenberg School of Communications, University of Pennsylvania.

4. For example:
   L. Heath, L. B. Bresolin, and R. C. Rinaldi, "Effects of Media Violence on Children," *Archives of General Psychiatry* 46 (1989): 376–79.

5. G. Gerbner, "Children's Television: A National Disgrace," *Pediatric Annals* 14 (1985): 823.

6. For example:
   J. Mortimer, "How TV Violence Hits Kids," *Educational Digest* (October 1994) 16.

   W. Wood, F. Y. Wong, and G. J. Chachere, "Effects of Media Violence on Viewers' Aggression in Unconstrained Social Interaction," *Psychological Bulletin* 109 (1991) 371–83.

CHAPTER 3

1. Interview "Minds of Young Are Left in Turmoil," *The New York Times,* 25 April 1995.

2. G. P. Koocher, "Talking with Children About Death," *American Journal of Orthopsychiatry* 44 (1974): 409–11.

3. E. Mahan and D. Simpson, "The Painted Guinea Pig," *The Psychoanalytic Study of the Child* 32 (1977): 283–303.

4. M. Nagy, "The Child's Theories Concerning Death," *The Journal of Genetic Psychology* 73 (1948): 3–27.

5. A. Freud and D. Burlingham, *War and Children* (New York: International Universities Press, 1943).

CHAPTER 4

1. R. Massie and S. Massie, *Journey* (New York: Knopf, 1973) 14.

2. R. Massie and S. Massie, *Journey* (New York: Knopf, 1973) 94–95.

3. R. Massie and S. Massie, *Journey* (New York: Knopf, 1973) 167–68.

Dr. Janice Cohn, a psychotherapist, is Chief of Consultation and Education at the Department of Psychiatry, Newark Beth Israel Medical Center. She is also in private practice in New York City and in Montclair, New Jersey. Dr. Cohn is the author of the following books for children: *I Had a Friend Named Peter: Talking to Children About the Death of a Friend*; *Why Did It Happen? Helping Children Cope in a Violent World*; *Molly's Rosebush*, a story about miscarriage; and *The Christmas Menorahs: How a Town Fought Hate*. Dr. Cohn lives in Montclair, New Jersey.